An Hachette UK Company
www.hachette.co.uk

First published in the United Kingdom in 2022
by Ilex, an imprint of
Octopus Publishing Group Ltd
Carmelite House
50 Victoria Embankment
London EC4Y 0DZ
www.octopusbooks.co.uk
www.octopusbooksusa.com

Distributed in the US by Hachette Book Group
1290 Avenue of the Americas, 4th & 5th Floors,
New York, NY 101014

Distributed in Canada by Canadian Manda Group
664 Annette Street, Toronto, Ontario,
Canada M6S 2C8

Publisher: Alison Starling
Commissioning Editor: Ellie Corbett
Managing Editor: Rachel Silverlight
Editorial Assistant: Ellen Sandford O'Neill
Art Director: Ben Gardiner
Design: Studio Polka
Layout: Tammy Kerr
Photographer: Kim Lightbody
Illustrator: Caitlin Keegan
Stylist: Rachel Vere
Production Managers: Lucy Carter and Nic Jones

ISBN 978-1-78157-823-0

A CIP catalogue record for this book is available
from the British Library.

Printed and bound in China

10 9 8 7 6 5 4 3 2 1

YOU WILL BE ABLE TO MACRAMÉ BY THE END OF THIS BOOK

TIFFANY ALLEN

ilex

Introduction

Knot and Technique Library

Projects

Learning to macramé

Macramé is back and better than ever! Perhaps you've seen modern macramé art popping up all over the place, which has led you to this book. It hasn't taken long for people to see the beauty in fibre art and it's now on display in chic boutiques, swanky hotels, corporate offices, beauty salons, wedding venues … the list goes on. Social media shows this trend is on the rise, with photos of beautifully styled interiors with walls and windows decorated in modern fibre art.

Macramé is an age-old craft that uses knots and knotting techniques to create a variety of decorative textiles. Macramé-style knots have been used for decoration all over the world and throughout history. Arab weavers are known to have adorned fabric with ornamental knots in the 13th century; they were added to tablecloths, clothing and curtains in Victorian-era Europe; and the same knots used for this craft were used by sailors for centuries to make hammocks, belts and other practical items during their sea voyages. Some of us lived through the last contemporary resurfacing of macramé in the 1970s, but the decorative handmade items that we are seeing today are quite different to what was around 50 years ago, and in my opinion, the state of the craft is the best that it has ever been. The vast range of materials that are available today allows makers to really get creative and to experiment with interesting textures and colours.

My macramé journey began back in 2016 with a ball of yarn and driftwood that I had collected from the shores of Lake Superior, Ontario, during a family outing. I had seen photographs of macramé wall hangings that were styled in stunning bohemian-inspired interiors and I was immediately attracted to the intricate patterns and the use of all-natural materials such as wood, cotton, jute and wool.

I was eager to get started on my first project and began researching some basic knots and techniques for making a wall hanging. As I began tying the knots, I realized that I already knew how to tie square knots and hitches. At that moment, memories from my childhood came rushing back and right away I remembered where I had learned how to do it. When I was around eight years old, a friend from elementary school taught me how to make different styles of friendship bracelets with the same knots that are used in macramé. When the recess bell rang at school,

my friends and I would rush outside and sit ourselves down on a grassy area to work on our bracelets together as a group. I find it quite remarkable that a hobby I enjoyed so much as a child has taken on a new form in my adulthood and is something that I have once again fallen in love with.

Fast forward a few years from my first wall hanging, and I have turned my favourite pastime and creative outlet into a thriving business that allows me to make handmade pieces for myself, my friends and family, and wonderful customers from around the world. I have become part of a community of makers and now teach others about this craft. This mindful and relaxing activity has brought so much joy to my life and I am so grateful that I gave myself the time to learn and to practise it. I am thrilled to be able to share my knowledge of macramé with you, and I hope that you will experience the same enjoyment that I do when working on a project.

Macramé is really quite simple to pick up once you have learned a few of the basic knots and techniques that allow you to create different patterns. In this book I will be sharing modern designs to accent your home, and some practical and wearable lifestyle pieces that you will be able to use every day. This book has been written for absolute beginners who have no experience with macramé, but it can also be enjoyed by seasoned fibre artists who would like to learn some new patterns.

As you make your way through the book, you will learn the basics of materials, tools, knots and techniques in order to successfully complete all of the projects. And once you have worked your way through it, you will be an expert at tying knots and you will be able to move on to creating your own beautiful designs. Macramé is a mindful practice that allows you to slow down and focus on a task and to really be present in the moment. For this reason, it is a calming and peaceful activity that you can enjoy while spending time with yourself. I'm excited to share this craft with you and I know that, once you get started, you will be passionate about it, too.

Tiffany
@macrameanddriftwood

Getting set up

The first thing to decide before you begin is where you are going to work on your macramé projects. You should choose an area of your home that you will enjoy spending time in and where you are able to move about freely. Some of the projects in this book will take several hours to complete, so make sure that you are in a setting where you feel comfortable and inspired. The space should have good lighting so you are not straining your eyes when reading the instructions and looking at your work. A small side table or stool nearby is helpful for laying down your tools and this book when not in use. If you enjoy listening to music or burning candles, then go ahead and set that up as well to add to the ambience in the room. Macramé can be a very relaxing and mindful activity. Be patient with yourself as you learn the different knots and techniques and remember to enjoy the process.

Learning how to do macramé can be physically demanding, especially when you are working on larger-sized projects. It is going to take some time for your body to get used to all of the new movements, so please remember to take frequent breaks and allow yourself to rest if you are feeling tired or stiff. Remember that stretching your muscles will prevent them from shortening and becoming tight, and it will help to improve your range of motion. Be kind to your body, go slow, and drink plenty of fluids to stay hydrated.

Be patient with yourself
as you learn the different
knots and techniques
and remember to enjoy
the process.

VERTICAL SETUP

Most of the projects in this book are easiest to tackle with a setup that allows the cords to hang down vertically. Having the cords hanging down and side by side will prevent them from tangling and will keep the project level as you work on it. If you plan to do macramé as a hobby and do not mind investing in your setup, then I highly recommend purchasing a garment rack to use for your craft; if you can find one that has an option to adjust the height of the hanging rod, even better. Some garment racks come with an expandable hanging rod that will be useful for larger projects. Alternatively, you can use a stable curtain rod, closet rod, wall hooks, or even a chair or two to hold your project up while you work on it. I encourage you to take a few minutes to look around your home to see what you may already have that could work before you run out and purchase anything new. Whichever option you choose for your setup, make sure that it is safe and that it will hold the weight of the materials that you will use for your projects.

When it comes to hanging your project from your chosen rod or bar, I recommend two sturdy S-hooks that have a large enough opening to hold the driftwood or dowels that you will be using. If you are unable to find suitable S-hooks, then you could use two pieces of rope to tie your project onto the rod – just make sure that both sides will hang evenly.

Most of the projects in this book can be done while standing, but as you work your way from top to bottom you may want to take a seat on a chair or a stool in order to keep your eyes in line with the section that you are working on. When I first learned macramé, I used to sit on a small wooden stool and then later on I upgraded to a comfortable office chair with an adjustable seat. You may end up sitting or kneeling on the floor for some of the projects and might find it helpful to have some cushioning for your knees such as a pillow, folded blanket or a kneeling pad.

FLAT WORKING SURFACE

A few of the smaller projects in this book can be done on a flat working surface such as a table or a desk. Taking the weight off your feet for a little while and having a comfortable place to sit will help to make the entire experience more enjoyable. You will need a way to keep proper and consistent tension on the cords that you are working with when your project is lying on a horizontal surface, so here are a few different approaches that I have found helpful when working on some of the small macramé items.

For small projects, you can use a cork board or cork trivet and pins to hold the project in place as you work on it. Pins with a ball or flat head are easiest to push into the cork, and are gentle on your fingertips. The board or trivet should have enough weight to hold the project down on the table or desk as you work on it and should be thick enough for the pins to stay in. I find that when I am working on plant rugs or mug rugs, it is easier to turn the board or trivet around in a circular motion rather than adjusting the pins and project as I work my way around the circumference of the pattern.

Clamps are another helpful tool for holding your projects in place. Spring clamps are nice because they are quick to install, they come in a variety of sizes, they are easy to find at a local hardware store, and they are relatively inexpensive. Trigger clamps and clutch-style clamps are also great options.

For some projects, a clipboard can be used, with the strong clip at the top securing the cords or hardware of your project in place while you work on it. A cork clipboard is ideal, as you can also fasten projects onto it with pins.

Your horizontal workspace does not need to be large and you will only need enough room for the project and the hanging cords, a measuring tape or ruler, a pair of scissors or shears, and possibly a cork trivet or cork board and your pins. I usually keep my roll of string or rope on the floor beside me, since it is easier to pull new rope when it is a few feet below my hands.

When working on some projects, such as the Feathers project in this book, you will be doing a lot of brushing with either a fine-toothed comb or a wire-bristle brush, so it is best to choose a surface that is resistant to scratches. You could also brush out the cords on top of a book, magazine, piece of cardboard or cutting mat if you are worried about scratches.

Tools

One of many perks of learning macramé is that very few tools are needed. The setup for my first wall hanging was a piece of driftwood tied onto the back of an old wooden chair. Over the years I have really streamlined how I work, but still the price for my ideal setup definitely does not break the bank. I am going to save you the time of having to figure it out on your own by sharing what I've found works best for me.

CUTTING

The most essential tool is a good pair of scissors or shears. Macramé involves cutting a lot of rope, and being able to cut through it easily and cleanly is going to save you a lot of time and energy. Over the years, I have found that scissors and shears that have only metal parts are the most durable and will hold up against the thicker rope that you will sometimes be cutting through. I recommend that you steer clear of anything that has plastic components, as they tend to break when you are cutting through thicker ropes or bundles with multiple cords. Choose a pair with a sharp, pointy tip for precise cuts and for getting into hard-to-reach spaces. I encourage you to spend the extra money and invest in a good set of scissors or shears that are comfortable to use and will last many years.

A rotary cutter and a cutting mat are two luxury items in the world of macramé. You definitely do not need to run out and purchase either of these items; however, if you do, you will not be disappointed. In my opinion, a rotary cutter is the best way to get flawless cuts across a row of cords or a brushed-out fringe. Cutting mats usually have measurements and a grid on them, so you can easily line up your cords or a fringe to the proper measurement before you start cutting. I also recommend using a ruler with these tools so that you can roll the rotary cutter along the straight edge of the ruler to get a perfectly straight cut. Rotary cutters also come in handy for trimming the fringe around circular items such as a mug rug or a plant rug and can quickly remove the fuzzy ends on a fringe after it has been brushed out with a comb.

MEASURING

You will need a tape measure or a ruler for all of the projects in this book. I prefer to use a tape measure for measuring long pieces of rope and a 30-cm (12-in) ruler for measuring smaller pieces of rope or for measuring spacing in the patterns.

BRUSHING

Some of the projects in this book instruct you to brush out the cords with a fine-toothed comb to create a fluffy and full fringe. You do not need anything fancy and can simply use an inexpensive comb that you may already have in your bathroom. I prefer a comb with teeth that are closely spaced on one half and a little more widely spaced on the other side. This way, I can begin by brushing out the cords using the wider-spaced teeth and finish with the other side of the comb, which can help to prevent tangling. A wire-bristle brush can also be used.

HOT GLUE

While not absolutely necessary, a hot glue gun designed for arts and crafts can certainly come in handy in macramé projects. In the Knot and Technique Library section of the book I will teach you how to tie a Hanger String (see page 65) and I recommend the use of hot glue. I like to glue the cut ends of the Hanger String down to the dowel or driftwood to keep the knots looking tidy and to hold them in place. Hot glue dries very quickly and has an immediate strong bond. If you choose to use a glue gun, please use it carefully and follow the manufacturer's guidelines.

MASK

Working with materials such as rope, string and yarn can sometimes cause tiny fibres to become airborne. For this reason, you may wish to wear a mask or face covering if you find that the fibres are tickling the tip of your nose.

Materials

In this section I will be walking you through the materials that you will need for the projects in this book, as well as some fundamental information about other supplies that you may wish to use for future projects.

TWISTED ROPE

Twisted rope is usually made by twisting two or three bundles of many threads or strings together to create one rope. Each of the bundles has already been twisted, and then those bundles are plied together – you will often hear 'three-ply' or 'four-ply', which describes how many bundles of threads have been twisted together to make a rope. Twisted rope is durable and sturdy and works nicely for plant hangers, wall hangings, home décor and wearable items that require a little more stability, although it can be tough on the hands, so you will want to take regular breaks to give your hands a rest.

When the rope is cut, the strings will unravel easily – so it is best if you wrap the cut ends with a piece of tape before you start working with it. You can save yourself time by wrapping the rope with a piece of tape where the next cut will be, and then cut through the middle of the taped section so that both ends are taped closed after it has been cut.

When the rope is unravelled, the strings have a curly or wavy appearance, which adds beautiful texture to a project. The strings can also be brushed out to make a full and fluffy fringe if desired. Once you have finished your project, the tape that was wrapped around the cut ends can be removed and the rope will naturally unravel a little bit over time. If you want to prevent the rope on your finished project from unravelling, you can try keeping the ends wrapped in tape, applying a small dab of hot glue and pinching the ends together, tying small Gathering Knots around the ends with thread (see page 64) or dipping them into melted wax.

When purchasing twisted rope, you will have the option to choose the length of the rope or sometimes the weight of the roll, as well as the diameter of the rope, which is usually measured in millimetres.

SINGLE STRAND STRING

Single strand string can be used to make wall hangings, plant hangers, home décor and wearable items and it is one of the most common materials used in macramé today.

This type of string is made by twisting many threads or thin strands of fibre together into one bundle. The strands are usually wound loosely to create one uniform twisted string. Since the strands are loosely twisted together, it can be a little bit finicky to work with, as the fibres can snag more easily than those in tightly twisted rope. The strands will brush out easily to create a fringe, and that makes it the perfect material for tassels and macramé feathers. Single strand string has a smooth appearance, and it is usually soft and gentle on the hands.

When purchasing single strand string, you will have the option to choose the length of the rope or sometimes the weight of the roll, as well as the thickness of the string, which is usually measured in millimetres. Most of the projects in this book use single strand cotton string.

BRAIDED CORD

Though not used in this book, braided cord – also known as sash cord – is durable and sturdy and works nicely for plant hangers, home décor and some wearable items. This type of cord is made up of multiple threads or strings that have been braided together to form one larger strand. Braided cord is sold as either flat or round and it comes in a variety of designs that will be determined by the way that the strings have been braided together.

When braided cord is cut, it tends to hold together quite well and rarely frays when you are working with it; however, this also means that it is not ideal for brushed-out fringe or details.

This type of cord is usually sturdy and stiff and can be tough on the hands, so remember to take breaks to give your hands a rest. When purchasing braided cord, you will have the option to choose the length of the cord or sometimes the weight of the roll, as well as the thickness, which is usually measured in millimetres.

KNIT FABRIC YARN

This type of yarn is used less commonly in macramé, but if you do decide to give it a try you will not be disappointed. Knit fabric is made with one long yarn or thread that had been wound around itself over and over again to give a braided appearance. It is usually sold in tube form with a filler or as a flat, ribbon-like yarn. Smooth and stretchy, it is a comfortable material to work with. However, when working with stretchy yarn, you may find it difficult to keep proper tension throughout the project and you should take your time to make sure that the spacing in the pattern is consistent and correct. You may want to practise tying some knots with the yarn before you jump into a project.

When this type of yarn is cut it tends to hold quite well and rarely frays, even while you are working on a project. Knit fabric is not meant to be brushed out and I do not recommend that you try, as you will most likely end up damaging the material.

When purchasing knit fabric yarn, you will have the option to choose the length or sometimes the weight of the roll, as well as the thickness of the yarn, also known as the 'yarn weight'.

COMMON TYPES OF FIBRE USED IN MACRAMÉ

All of the projects in this book are made with plant-based cotton fibre. Cotton string and rope is the mainstay of modern macramé artwork, and it is one of the easiest materials to come by when looking for supplies. I personally enjoy working with plant- or animal-based fibres the best, as their natural qualities look beautiful in almost any setting.

COMMON FIBRES AND MATERIALS

PLANT	ANIMAL	SYNTHETIC
Cotton	Wool	Polyester
Jute	Silk	Acrylic
Bamboo		Nylon
Linen		
Hemp		

COMMON TYPES OF HARDWARE USED IN MACRAMÉ

Wood dowels

Wood boards

Metal hoops

Metal frames in various shapes

Wood rings

Metal rings

Keychain hardware

D-rings

Swivel clips

COMMON TYPES OF BEADS USED IN MACRAMÉ

Wood – natural and unfinished or painted or stained

Metal

Ceramic

Glass

Polymer clay

Semi-precious stones

PURCHASING SUPPLIES

For each of the projects in this book, I have specified the rope and string that I used so that you will be able to order the same or similar products. Unless you are purchasing exactly the same materials, I recommend ordering ten to fifteen percent more than the project requires to ensure that you have enough to complete it. Diameter measurements are not always consistent between suppliers: some suppliers measure the diameter of their rope when it is pulled tightly, and others measure it after it is off the spool and has had a chance to sit and relax. It's best to check with the supplier to ensure that you are ordering the right size for each of the projects; the chances of running out of rope too soon will be much lower, and any leftover pieces can be saved for future projects.

Something else to consider is that many manufacturers make their products in small batches, and the same type of rope in the same colour from the same supplier may be a little bit different from one batch to another. Suppliers also tend to change their colours often and they can sell out very quickly. Signing up for email newsletters to receive alerts about new products, restocks and promotions can be helpful. If you are not sure if a particular product will work for your project, or if you want to see and handle the rope before you purchase it, most suppliers are more than happy to send out samples of their products.

CALCULATING HOW MUCH ROPE TO USE

When it comes to working out how much rope to use for your own projects, unfortunately there is no 'one size fits all' answer. The amount of cord that you will need depends greatly on the intricacies of the design, how tightly you tie your knots and the thickness of your rope. There are, however, a few approaches that I use when calculating how much rope to use for projects and you can decide which one will work best for your project.

If you will be making a design that is repetitive from top to bottom, then making a sample will help you determine the amount of rope that you will need to finish the whole pattern. For instance, if you were planning on making a design with a column of diamond shapes in it, then you can see how much rope it takes to make one diamond and multiply this amount by the total number of diamonds in the pattern. In order to do this, fasten the ropes onto your dowel or driftwood and measure the length of the cords that are hanging vertically. Make one of the diamond shapes and then measure the remaining length of the cords after the sample is done. Subtract this from the original measurement to determine how much rope was used. Just remember that each of the ropes was folded in half before it was attached to the dowel, so this measurement must be doubled, and that you may also need to include additional lengths for attaching the ropes to the dowel and for a fringe along the bottom, if included.

For example, if your cords measured 30cm (12in) long after they were attached to a dowel and 10cm (4in) remained after the sample diamond shape was made, then that means that the diamond shape uses 40cm (16in) per rope (20cm/8in x 2 per cord). If you were planning on making a column of six diamonds, then the ropes would have to be 240cm/96in (40cm/16in x 6) plus any extra lengths.

If you are planning to make a design that is not repetitive, then the process suggested above will not work. Though it's not a perfect method, I have found that you can usually multiply the expected length of your design by nine to find your rope length, when working on intricate patterns where the knots are tied closely together. For example, if you want the design to be 30cm (1ft) long, then you would cut the ropes 270cm (9ft) long, plus extra to wrap around the dowel or driftwood, and any fringe detail to be included. For patterns that have a decent amount of spacing between the knots, you can multiply the length by six to find your rope length.

I also find it helpful to look back at previous projects that have a similar design or similar spacing between knots to help decide how long to cut the ropes. Remember that it is always better to have too much rope than too little.

LEFTOVER PIECES OF ROPE

As you work your way through the projects section of this book, you are going to start accumulating small pieces of rope that are left over after you have made the final cuts to finish each of the projects. Hold on to all of your cuttings and keep them sorted in bundles of the same colour, and then again in groups of similar lengths. You will be able to use these smaller pieces to make feathers, tassels, mug rugs, plant rugs, Gathering Knots, or to make a fringe on a wall hanging or a plant hanger. Really short pieces that you are not able to use can be given to another crafter who may be able to use them in different projects. Spinners, for example, are able to make beautiful and unique art yarn by spinning smaller pieces of cotton rope and string with wool roving and other materials.

Knot and

Technique Library

Using the library

In this section, I will teach you how to tie the most common knots used in macramé, which you will be able to use in your own designs long after you have finished the projects in this book. Once you are familiar with tying the various knots, you will be able to move through the patterns more quickly. After completing a few projects, you might not even have to think about which cord loops around and behind the other, because your hands will automatically know what to do. It is truly amazing to me how quickly some people are able to learn this craft. I encourage you to practise the different knots before you dive into a project, as this will help to boost your confidence before getting started.

Essential terms

Before you get started, there are some terms that you will need to know in order to understand the instructions.

TENSION

In order for the knots to hold and to be worked into a pattern, you will need to tie them with the proper amount of tension. As you learn how to tie the various knots, you will start to understand what proper tension looks and feels like.

Your knots should be tight enough to hold their shape and to look like the pictures. They should be snug, but not so tight that they become misshaped or start to alter the design around them. You will be able to see fairly quickly if your knots are being pulled too tightly or too loosely. If you tie them too loosely, then the design will look a little bit messy – but if you pull them too tight, then it is going to affect the overall shape of the project. As you gain more experience with tying the various knots, proper tension will come naturally to you. Strive for symmetry and an overall clean look.

ROPE

For the purposes of this book, I will use the term 'rope' to mean the lengths of material that are cut before the project begins, before they have been secured to a dowel, ring or rope.

CORD (C)

For the purposes of this book, a 'cord' refers to a length of cut rope that has been secured to the dowel, ring or rope, ready to be worked into the pattern. Cords will be identified with the letter C and then labelled with a number in sequence starting from the left and moving to the right. For example, Cord 1 (C1) will be the farthest cord on the left side, Cord 2 (C2) will be to the right of Cord 1 (C1), Cord 3 (C3) will be to the right of Cord 2 (C2), and so on. See the diagram for clarification.

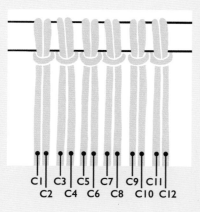

C1 C2 C3 C4 C5 C6 C7 C8 C9 C10 C11 C12

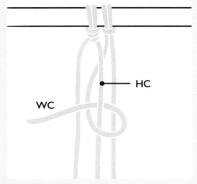

WORKING CORD (WC)
& HOLDING CORD (HC)

WORKING CORD (WC)

This is the cord that you are using to tie the various knots. The Working Cords are usually the cords that you will see forming the patterns.

HOLDING CORD (HC)

This is the cord that the Working Cords are fastened on to and the knots are tied around. Usually, you are just holding onto this cord.

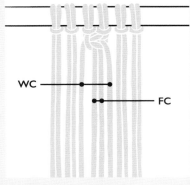

WORKING CORD (WC)
& FILLER CORD (FC)

FILLER CORD (FC)

This is the cord or cords that knots are tied around. These cords usually end up inside and hidden under the Working Cords.

FRINGE

A fringe is made up of decorative cords that create a border of strings that hang loosely. For some of the projects, you will simply attach the cords and leave them as they are; for other projects, you will brush the cords out.

SINNET

This is a column that is formed by tying a series of knots, one directly after the other. It may be flat in appearance, for example, if it is formed by tying multiple Square knots (SQ) one after the other using the same cords (see page 36). It may also twist or spiral, if it is formed by tying Half-Square knots (HSQ) one after the other using the same cords (see pages 34–5). Some of the sinnets that you will make in this book are made up of a variety of knots that are all in the same column and form a chain.

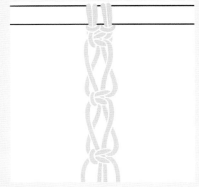

SINNET

DOWNWARD DIAGONAL LINE (DDL)

Describes the direction that a series of knots will follow when working on a pattern. The sequence of knots will gradually move in a downward and diagonal direction, either from left to right or from right to left.

HANGER STRING (HS)

A rope that is fastened on to a dowel, driftwood, metal ring, wood ring or rope, etc. and is used to hang the item up. The project will hang from this string in order to display it.

ROW

A sequence of knots that form a horizontal line. The first horizontal line of knots across the top of the pattern is defined as the First Row or Row One. The second horizontal line of knots from the top is defined as the Second Row or Row Two. The third row from the top is defined as the Third Row or Row Three, and so on.

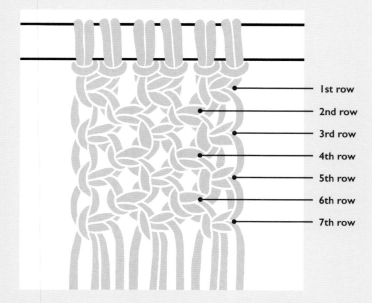

1st row
2nd row
3rd row
4th row
5th row
6th row
7th row

PANEL

A patterned section of knots within a larger design that is separated from the other section(s).

WARP

A series of cords side by side that run vertically. They are held in place with some tension at the top and bottom, usually using a series of knots on both ends.

Knots

This section introduces you to the knots we will be using in the projects, and are worth practising until you're familiar with each one. When tying the various knots, try to avoid rubbing the cords against each other, as friction on the material can cause damage, especially when working with single strand cotton.

Loop

In order to make some of the projects in this book, you will need to know how to make a Loop to get the patterns started.

Step 1: Cut a piece of rope to the desired length. Lay one of the ends down on a flat working surface.

Step 2: Hold the end in place and then pick up the other side of the rope and make a circle approx. 8cm (3in) in diameter that goes in an anti-clockwise direction. The long end of the rope should be on the right and the short end should be 2–4cm (¾–1½in) to the left of the Loop.

Overhand Loop Knot (OLK)

This is a very common knot that you have most likely already tied at some point. This knot is used in a couple of the projects to attach a piece of rope to hang your wall hanging or garland from.

Step 1: Cut a piece of rope to the desired length. Fold the rope in half, line up the cut ends and then lay the folded rope down on a flat working surface. In this example, the cut ends are on the right and the folded end on the left.

Step 2: Bring the folded end of the rope up and around towards the middle of the rope and then down and over the top.

Step 3: Bring the folded end underneath the cords and then up through the loop.

Step 5: Once the knot is in the correct position, pull on both ends to tighten it. Trim the cut ends to shorten them and clean them up, if you like.

Step 4: Gently pull on the folded end of the rope while moving the knot into the desired position.

Overhand Knot (OK)

This is very simple, and you probably already know how to tie one of these. In macramé, these knots are usually tied in pairs, one on top of the other, since a single Overhand Knot will not hold very well.

Step 1: Cut a piece of rope to the desired length.

Step 2: Place the left end over and across the right end of the rope.

Step 3: Bring the upper end down behind the lower end and back up out through the circle.

Step 4: Gently pull on both ends of the rope while moving the knot into the desired position.

KNOT AND TECHNIQUE LIBRARY

Lark's Head (LH)

This knot is typically used to attach rope to a dowel, a piece of driftwood, a ring or another piece of rope. It is often used at the beginning of a project or to attach ropes to make a fringe.

Step 1: Cut a piece of rope to the desired length. Fold the rope in half.

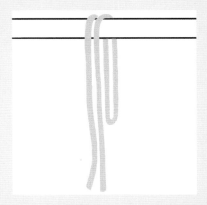

Step 2: Place the folded end over and behind the supporting dowel, rope or ring.

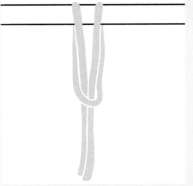

Step 3: Bring the cut ends back through the folded end of the rope.

Step 4: Pull tight and position so that the cords hang straight down.

Two Lark's Head knots with one rope

This technique is typically used when you require a supporting rope to hold additional ropes for a project. This is often used to add layers or a fringe to a project.

Step 1: Start by tying a Lark's Head (LH) with your rope, leaving the desired amount of cord hanging from either side.

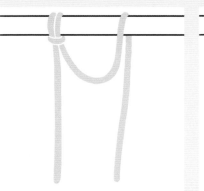

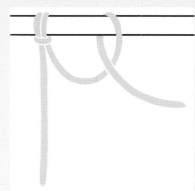

Step 2: Take the end of the rope that will form the second LH. Put the rope over and behind the supporting dowel, rope or ring.

Step 3: Bring the end of the rope over and across the rope on the front side.

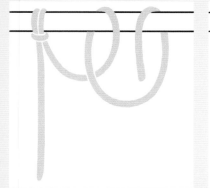

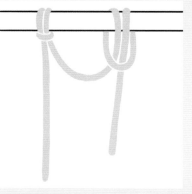

Step 4: Bring the rope behind the supporting dowel, rope or ring and then up and over the top to create a U-shape.

Step 5: Bring the end down through the U-shape.

Step 6: Pull tight and position so that the cords hang straight down. Trim the ends level if desired.

Reverse Lark's Head (RLH)

This knot is typically used to attach rope to a dowel, a piece of driftwood, a ring or another piece of rope. It is often used at the beginning of a project or to attach ropes to make a fringe. It is exactly the same as the Lark's Head knot, it just goes the other way around.

Step 1: Cut a piece of rope to the desired length. Fold the rope in half.

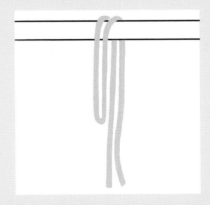

Step 2: Place the folded end over and in front of the supporting dowel, rope or ring.

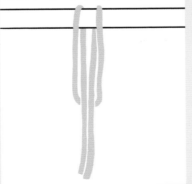

Step 3: Bring the cut ends through the folded end of the rope.

Step 4: Pull tight and position so that the cords hang straight down.

Half Square (HSQ)

This knot is typically used to create a twisted sinnet for plant hangers and wall hangings and it is one half of the Square knot (see page 36). The direction of the resulting spiral pattern will depend on whether you tie a Left Facing Half Square (LHSQ) or a Right Facing Half Square (RHSQ). It involves four cords hanging down, and can be practised by using two ropes and tying two Lark's Head knots close together.

**LEFT FACING HALF
SQUARE (LHSQ)**

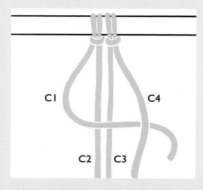

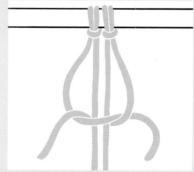

Step 1: Bring C1 over and across C2 and C3 and underneath C4.

Step 2: Bring C4 under and behind C2 and C3 and up through C1 and C2.

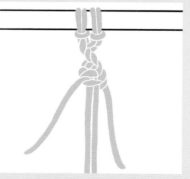

Step 3: Pull the ends of C1 and C4 to move the knot to the desired position and to tighten it to finish the knot.

Step 4: You can continue to tie Left Facing Half Squares (LHSQ) to create a twisted sinnet.

KNOT AND TECHNIQUE LIBRARY

RIGHT FACING HALF SQUARE (RHSQ)

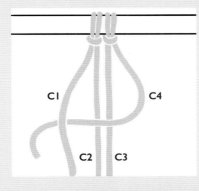

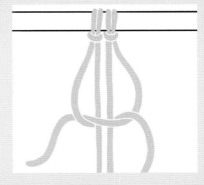

Step 1: Bring C4 over and across C3 and C2 and underneath C1.

Step 2: Bring C1 under and behind C2 and C3 and up through C3 and C4.

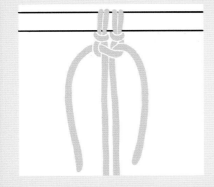

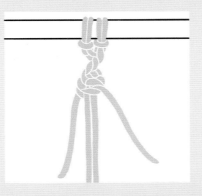

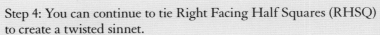

Step 3: Pull the ends of C1 and C4 to move the knot to the desired position and to tighten it to finish the knot.

Step 4: You can continue to tie Right Facing Half Squares (RHSQ) to create a twisted sinnet.

Square (SQ)

You will use the Square knot often in your macramé projects and it is typically used to create a pattern or a sinnet. This knot is made by tying a Left Facing Half Square and a Right Facing Half Square (see pages 34 and 35), one directly above the other, to form a square shape. You can create a sinnet by tying a series of Squares, one below the other.

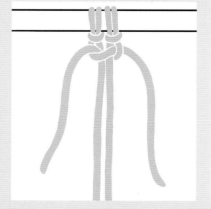

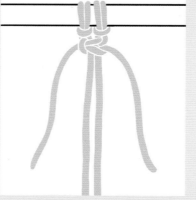

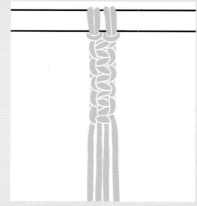

Step 1: Make a Left Facing Half Square (LFSQ).

Step 2: Make a Right Facing Half Square (RHSQ) directly below the LHSQ that you just made. This completes the Square (SQ)

Step 3: You can continue to tie SQs one below the other to form a sinnet.

Alternating Square (ASQ)

Like the basic Square (see page 36), Alternating Squares are one of the most common knotting techniques that you will use when doing macramé, and this pattern is used for a number of projects in this book. This technique uses at least two rows of Square knots and the rows are attached together.

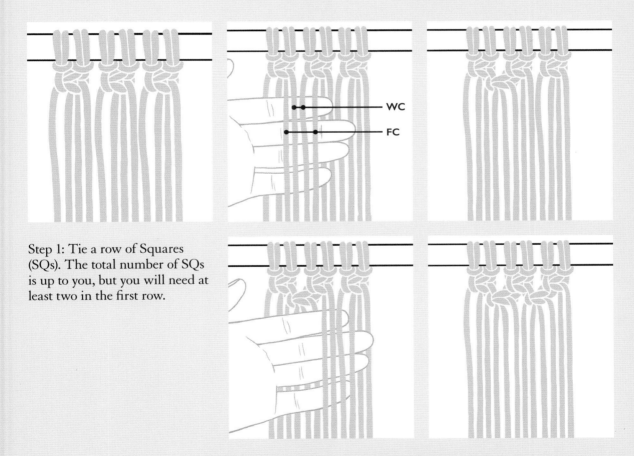

Step 1: Tie a row of Squares (SQs). The total number of SQs is up to you, but you will need at least two in the first row.

Step 2: Tie a second row of SQs using a Filler Cord (FC) and Working Cord (WC) from each of the SQs above. The second row of SQs should be centred between two SQs in the row above. The first two cords and the last two cords in the second row will not be used.

Alternating Square (ASQ)

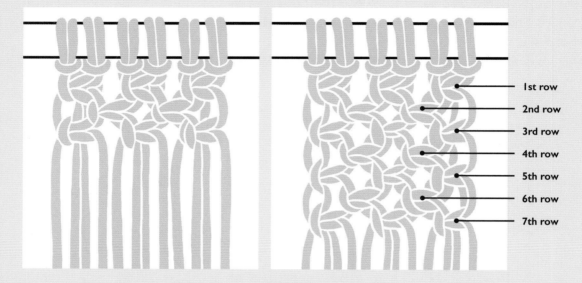

1st row
2nd row
3rd row
4th row
5th row
6th row
7th row

Step 3: Tie a third row of SQs using the same sets of cords that were used in the first row. The third row of SQs will be identical to the first row.

Step 4: Continue the pattern to create multiple rows of Alternating Squares (ASQs).

Alternating Square with spacing

This technique is identical to tying Alternating Squares, except that you will leave a space in between the rows. This pattern uses at least two rows of Alternating Squares and each of the rows have equal spaces between them.

Step 1: Tie a row of Squares (SQs). The total number of SQs is up to you, but you will need at least two in the first row.

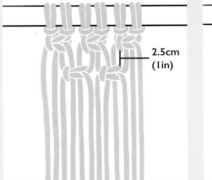

Step 2: Tie a second row of Alternating Squares (ASQs), leaving a space between the bottom of the first row and the top of the knots in the second row. In this example, we will leave a 2.5-cm (1-in) space between the rows.

Step 3: Tie a third row of ASQs, again leaving a 2.5-cm (1-in) space between the bottom of the second row and the top of the knots in the third row.

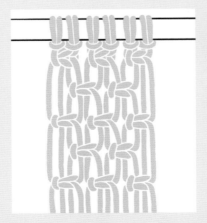

Step 4: Continue the pattern, leaving a 2.5-cm (1-in) space between the rows.

Decreasing Alternating Squares

This technique is identical to tying Alternating Squares (see page 37), except that you will be leaving out cords in each new row so that the pattern gradually decreases. This pattern uses at least two rows of Alternating Squares.

Step 1: Tie a row of Squares (SQs). The total number of SQs is up to you, but you will need at least two in the first row.

Step 2: Tie a second row of Alternating Squares (ASQs).

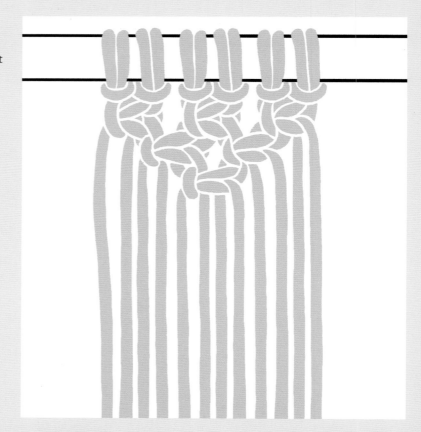

Step 3: Repeat the pattern, leaving out two more cords on each side with each row, until there is only one knot in the middle of the row, to finish the decreasing pattern. In this example, there are three knots in the first row, two in the second and one in the third.

Decreasing Open Alternating Squares

This technique is used to create a V-shape of knots, where the inside of the V-shape is left open and knot free. This example uses eight ropes (sixteen hanging cords) to make a total of four rows, but you can modify the number according to the size of your project.

Step 1: Start by tying Squares (SQs) with the first four cords and the last four cords, or the cords specified in the pattern instructions.

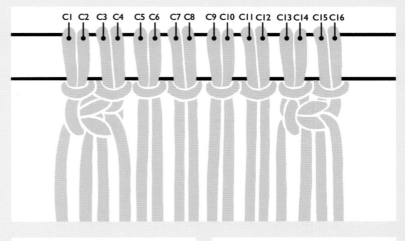

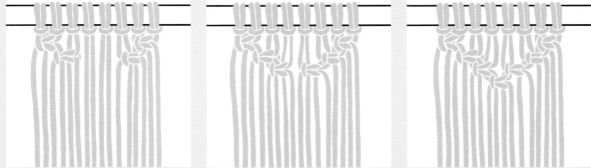

Step 2: Skip the first two cords in the second row and tie an Alternating Square (ASQ) using C3–6. Skip the last two cords in the second row and tie an ASQ using C11–14.

Step 3: Skip the first four cords in the third row and tie an ASQ using C5–8. Skip the last four cords in the third row and tie an ASQ using C9–12.

Step 4: Tie an ASQ using the middle cords of the fourth row (C7–10) to close the V-shape.

Increasing Alternating Squares

This technique is identical to tying Alternating Squares (see page 37), except that you will be gradually increasing the number of knots in each row. This pattern uses at least two rows of Alternating Squares and all the rows will all be attached. The example here uses six ropes (twelve cords) to make a total of three rows, but you can modify the number according to the size of your project.

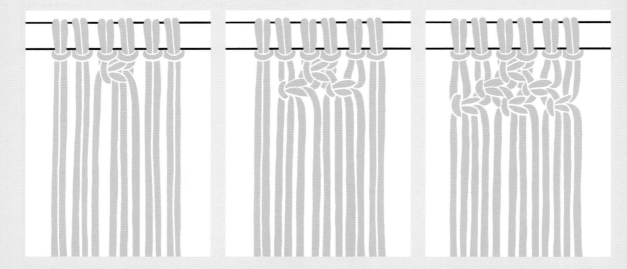

Step 1: Start by tying a Square (SQ) using the four middle cords, or the cords specified in the pattern instructions.

Step 2: Tie a second row of two Alternating Squares (ASQs) below the first row, adding in two cords on the right and two cords on the left.

Step 3: Tie a third row of three ASQs, adding in two cords on the right and two on the left.

Increasing Open Alternating Squares

This technique is used to create an upside-down V-shape of knots, where the inside is left open and knot free. This example uses eight ropes (sixteen hanging cords) to make a total of four rows, but you can modify the number according to the size of your project.

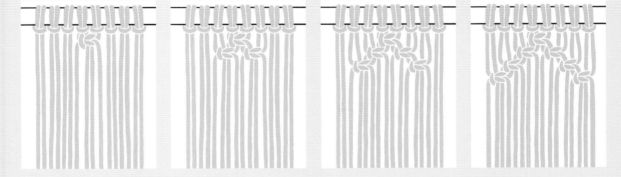

Step 1: Start by tying a Square (SQ) using the four middle cords, or the cords specified in the instructions for the pattern.

Step 2: Tie a second row of Alternating Squares (ASQs), adding in two cords on the right and two cords on the left.

Step 3: Tie two ASQs in the third row, again adding in two cords on the right and two cords on the left to continue the upside-down V-shape pattern.

Step 4: Continue the pattern by tying two ASQs until you reach the last two cords on the right and left, or as the pattern specifies.

Cord Alternating Squares (CASQ)

Cord Alternating Squares are similar to Alternating Squares (see page 37) except that, when we take the cords from the row above, we switch each pair of cords around to create a twisted effect that makes an open and airy design in a wall hanging.

Step 1: Start by tying a row of Squares (SQs).

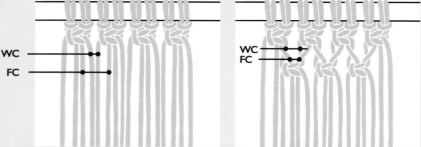

Step 2: Tie a second row of Alternating Squares (ASQs), keeping the Working Cords (WCs) from the first row as WCs in the second row and the Filler Cords (FCs) from the first row as FCs in the second row. You will not use the first two or last two cords in the second row.

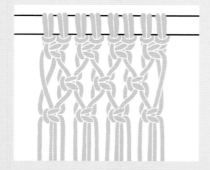

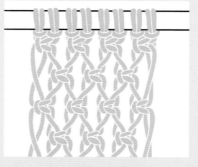

Step 3: Tie a third row of ASQs, using all the cords. The WCs from the first row become FCs in the third row and the FCs become WCs, but the WCs from the second row remain as WCs, and so on.

Step 4: Continue the pattern to the desired length.

Note: The spacing between the knots can dramatically affect the finished look. You can also use this technique to tie Decreasing or Increasing Cord Alternating Squares in your project.

KNOT AND TECHNIQUE LIBRARY

Cord Alternating Square Sinnet

You can also use a Cord Alternating Square to create a delicate-looking sinnet. When using only four cords to tie the knot straight down, we swap the Working Cords and Filler Cords around from row to row.

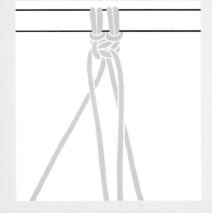 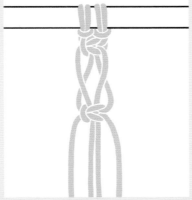 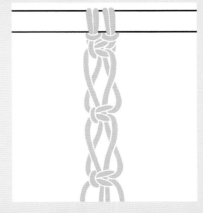

Step 1: Start by tying a Square knot (SQ).

Step 2: The Filler Cords (FCs) become the Working Cords (WCs) and the WCs become the FCs. Tie another SQ either directly below the first knot or spaced farther away.

Step 3: The FCs become the WCs and the WCs become the FCs. Tie another SQ either directly below the second one or spaced farther away. Continue the pattern until you reach the desired length.

Half Hitch (HH)

This knot is typically used to create one part of a Double Half Hitch (see page 48), or it can be used alone in a pattern. A series of these knots tied together can make a horizontal, vertical or diagonal line or it can be used to add a decorative element to a design. The direction of the line is guided by the position of the Holding Cord.

FROM LEFT TO RIGHT

Working from left to right, C1 is the Working Cord (WC) and C2 is the Holding Cord (HC).

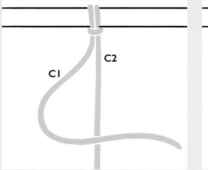

Step 1: Place C1 on top of and across C2 to create a number 4 shape.

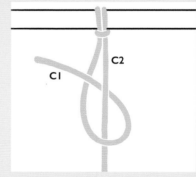

Step 2: Bring the end of C1 around and under C2, and then up and through the two cords.

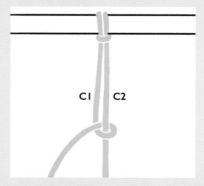

Step 3: Pull the end of C1 to the left to form an anti-clockwise loop around C2.

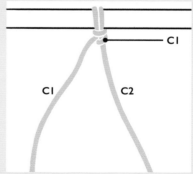

Step 4: Pull the loop up to the desired position and pull tight.

FROM RIGHT TO LEFT

Working from Right to Left, C2 is the Working Cord (WC) and C1 is the Holding Cord (HC).

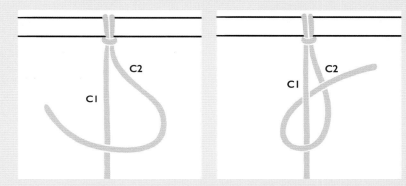

Step 1: Place C2 on top of and across C1 to create a backwards number 4 shape.

Step 2: Bring C2 around and under C1, and then up and through the two cords.

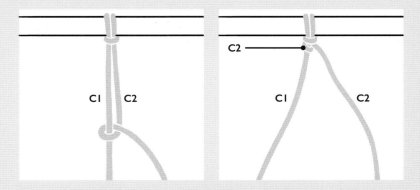

Step 3: Pull the end of C2 to the right to form a clockwise loop around C1.

Step 4: Pull the loop up to the desired position and pull tight.

Double Half Hitch (DHH)

This knot is typically used to create a linear segment. A series of these knots tied together can make a horizontal, vertical, diagonal or curved line or it can be used to add a decorative element to a design. The direction of the line is guided by the positioning of the Holding Cord.

FROM LEFT TO RIGHT

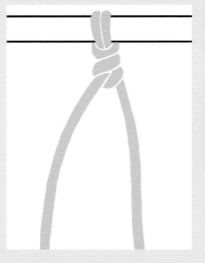

Step 1: Tie a left-to-right Half Hitch (HH).

Step 2: Repeat Steps 1–4 of the left-to-right HH instructions to finish the knot. Both loops should sit side by side and should be tight enough to hold the knot in place.

FROM RIGHT TO LEFT

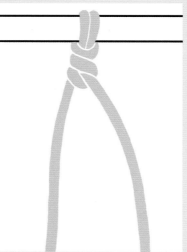

Step 1: Tie a right-to-left Half Hitch (HH).

Step 2: Repeat Steps 1–4 of the right-to-left HH instructions to finish the knot. Both loops should sit side by side and should be tight enough to hold the knot in place.

Adding cords with a Double Half Hitch

You can continue to add in cords to your linear segment by repeating the steps for the Double Half Hitch using the added cords. There is no limit on how many cords you can add into a project using this method, and it can be used to create a horizontal, vertical or diagonal line in your design.

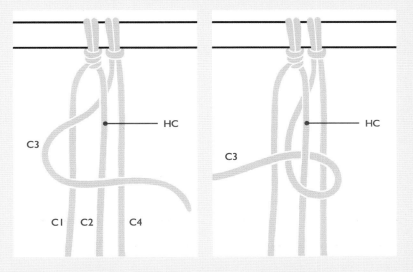

Step 1: The HC from the first DHH will remain the HC for the entire linear segment, and it will remain in front of the Working Cords (WCs) from this point on. Pick up the WC to the right (C3) and use it to make a number 4 shape that starts off behind the HC and then finishes in front.

Step 2: Bring the end of C3 around and under the HC and then up through the two cords to make a Half Hitch (HH).

Adding cords with a Double Half Hitch (DHH)

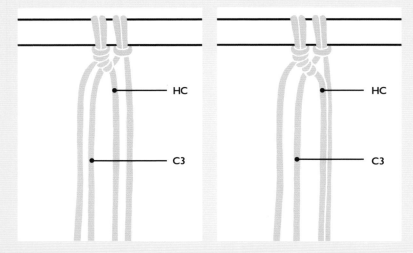

Step 3: Close the HH and slide it up so that it sits beside the first knot in the series.

Step 4: Tie one more HH using C3 to complete a DHH.

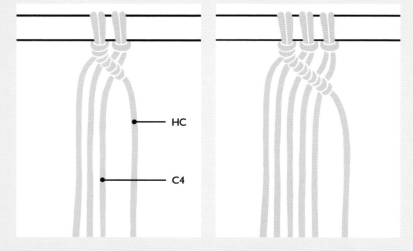

Step 5: Repeat the pattern using the next cord to the right (C4).

Step 6: Continue adding in cords using the same technique to form a linear segment of DHHs.

FROM RIGHT TO LEFT

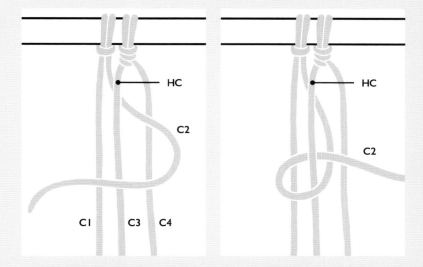

Step 1: The HC from the first DHH will remain the HC for the entire linear segment, and it will remain in front of the Working Cords (WCs) from this point on. Pick up the WC to the left (C2) and use it to make a backwards number 4 shape that starts off behind the HC and then finishes in front.

Step 2: Bring the end of C2 around and under the HC and then up through the two cords to make a Half Hitch (HH).

Continued from previous page

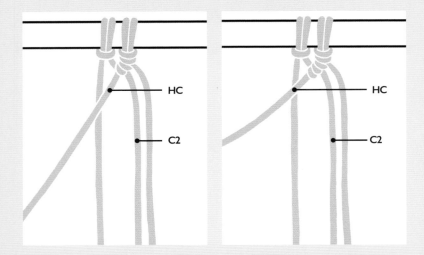

Step 3: Close the HH and slide it up so that it sits beside the first knot in the series.

Step 4: Tie one more HH using C2 to complete a DHH.

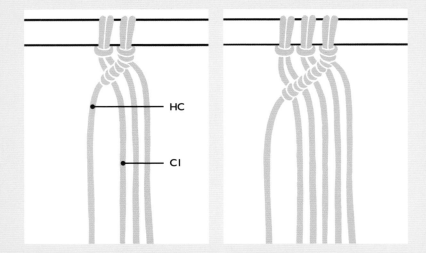

Step 5: Repeat the pattern using the next cord to the left (C1).

Step 6: Continue adding in cords using the same technique to form a linear segment of DHHs.

Double Half Hitch around a dowel or ring

This technique is used in the Intermediate Wall Hanging project (see page 106) and you may wish to do something similar in the future when you are coming up with your own original designs. Tying Double Half Hitch knots around a dowel creates a sleek and straight line in your design. This is a must if you insist on having long and perfectly straight lines in your projects.

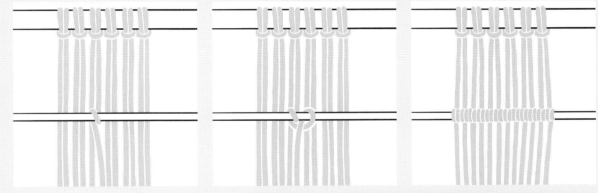

The ring or dowel will replace the Holding Cord (HC) in the Double Half Hitch (DHH). Use the Working Cords (WCs) to tie DHHs around the dowel or ring. The DHHs can be side by side or you can space them out along the dowel. You can start at either end, or in the middle of the dowel or ring. All of the knots should be tied tightly so that they hold the dowel in place.

Reverse Double Half Hitch (RDHH)

This knot is typically used to create a linear segment. A series of these knots tied together can make a horizontal, vertical, diagonal or curved line or it can be used to add a decorative element to a design. The direction of the line is guided by the positioning of the Holding Cord.

FROM LEFT TO RIGHT

Working from left to right, C2 is the Working Cord (WC) and C1 is the Holding Cord (HC).

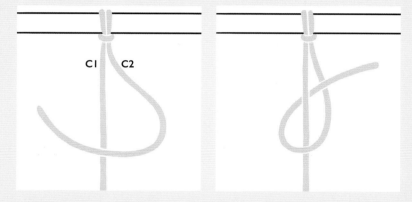

Step 1: Pick up the WC and use it to make a backwards number 4 shape that goes over and across the HC.

Step 2: Bring the end of the WC around and under the HC and then up through the two cords.

Tip: If you have mastered the Double Half Hitch (DHH), then you can simply turn the project over so that you are looking at the back side and then tie a DHH. Turn the project back over so that you are looking at the front side to reveal a Reverse Double Half Hitch (RDHH).

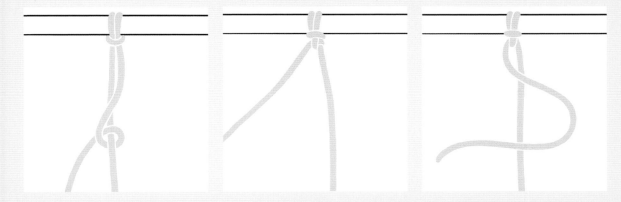

Step 3: Bring the WC to the left side and pull the loop up into position and close the knot.

Step 4: Bring the WC over and across the HC to make a backwards number 4 shape.

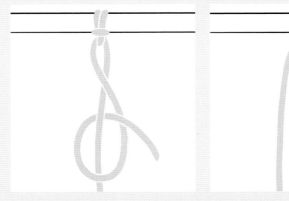

Step 5: Bring the end of the WC under the HC and then up through the two cords.

Step 6: Bring the WC to the left side and pull the loop up into position and close the knot.

Reverse Double Half Hitch (RDHH)

FROM RIGHT TO LEFT

Working from right to left, C1 is the Working Cord (WC) and C2 is the Holding Cord (HC).

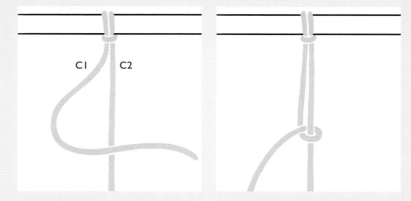

Step 1: Pick up the WC and use it to make a number 4 shape that goes over and across the HC.

Step 2: Bring the end of the WC around and under the HC, and then up and through the two cords.

Step 3: Bring the WC to the right side and pull the loop up into position and close the knot.

Step 4: Bring the WC over and across the HC to make a number 4 shape.

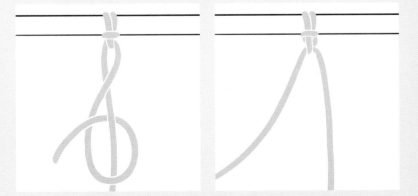

Step 5: Bring the end of the WC around and under the HC and then up through the two cords.

Step 6: Bring the WC to the right side and pull the loop up into position and close the knot.

Adding cords with a Reverse Double Half Hitch

You can continue to add cords to your linear segment by repeating the steps for the Reverse Double Half Hitch with the added cords. There is no limit on how many cords you can add into a project using this method.

FROM LEFT TO RIGHT

Once you have completed a Reverse Double Half Hitch (RDHH) that goes from left to right with the first rope (see page 54), you will begin to add the cords on the right into the pattern.

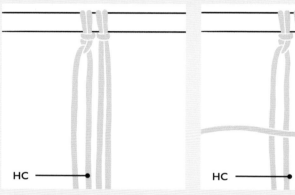

Step 1: The Holding Cord (HC) from the first knot will remain the HC for the entire linear segment, and it will remain in behind the Working Cords (WCs) from this point on.

Step 2: Pick up C3 and use it to make a backwards number 4 shape that goes over and across the HC.

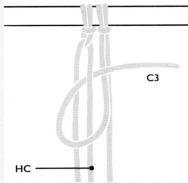

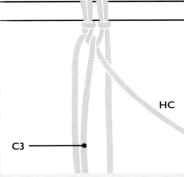

Step 3: Bring the end of C3 around and under the HC, and then up through the two cords.

Step 4: Bring C3 to the left side and pull the loop up into position and close the knot.

Step 5: Repeat Steps 2–4.

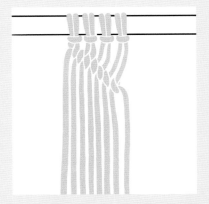

Step 6: Repeat the pattern with as many cords as you like to continue the linear segment.

Continued from previous page

Adding cords with a Reverse Double Half Hitch

FROM RIGHT TO LEFT

Once you have completed a Reverse Double Half Hitch (RDHH) that goes from right to left with the first rope (see page 56), you will begin to add the cords on the left side into the pattern.

C1 C2 C3 C4

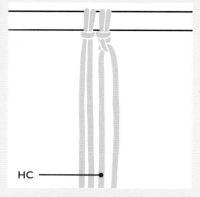

HC ———————•

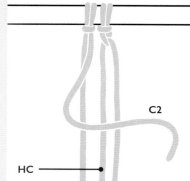

C2

HC ———————•

Step 1: The Holding Cord (HC) from the first knot will remain the HC for the entire linear segment, and it will remain in behind the Working Cords (WCs) from this point on.

Step 2: Pick up C2 and use it to make a number 4 shape that goes over and across the HC.

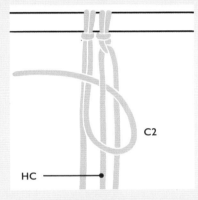

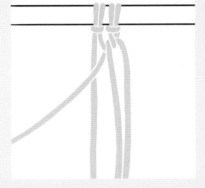

Step 3: Bring the end of C2 around and under the HC, and then up through the two cords.

Step 4: Bring C2 to the right side and pull the loop up into position and close the knot.

Step 5: Repeat Step 2–4.

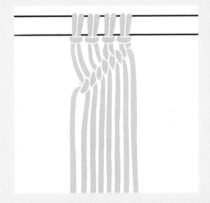

Step 6: Repeat the pattern with as many cords as you like to continue the linear segment.

Berry Knot (BK)

This knot looks just like the name describes it, a berry! This decorative little knot may look difficult to do but it is actually very simple, even for a beginner. You will use this knot in the Lamp Shade project (see page 132), and it can also be worked into your future wall hangings, plant hangers or other macramé accessories. The Berry Knot is made by tying a sinnet of Square knots (see page 36), rolling it into a ball shape and then securing it in place with another Square knot.

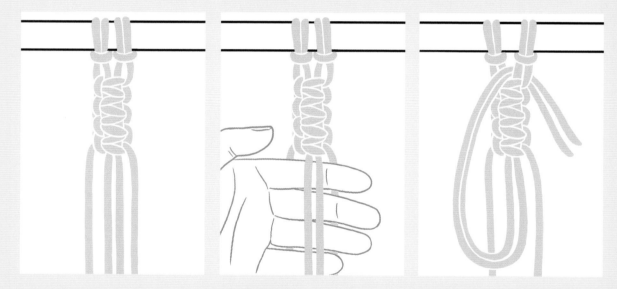

Step 1: You will require four cords: two Filler Cords (FCs) and two Working Cords (WCs). Use the four cords to make a sinnet of four Squares (SQ).

Step 2: Make a small space in between the second and third cords at the top of the sinnet. Separate the two FCs (C2 and C3).

Step 3: Pull the ends of the two FCs through the small space at the top of the sinnet, going from front to back.

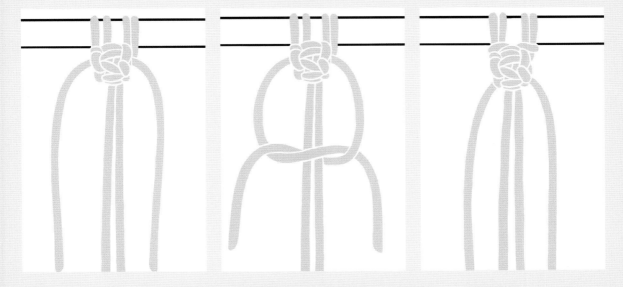

Step 4: Continue pulling the two FCs all the way through until the sinnet is rolled into a small ball shape.

Step 5: Tie a SQ directly below the ball to hold it in place.

Gathering Knot (GK)

This is typically used to tie a group of cords together, usually at the beginning and end of plant hangers, or at the end of a sinnet.

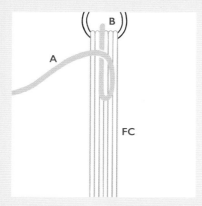

Step 1: Cut a piece of rope to the desired length. Neatly bundle the Filler Cords (FCs) together. Using the cut piece of rope, make a loop over the FCs as shown. The long end is A and the short end is B.

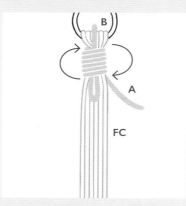

Step 2: Wrap the long end around the FCs as many times as the pattern suggests, starting at the top and working down. Leave the bottom of the loop unwrapped.

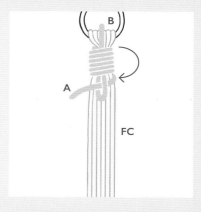

Step 3: Pass the end of A through the loop.

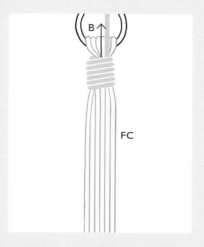

Step 4: Pull the short end of the cord (B) up until the loop is underneath the wrapped rope. If you have difficulty pulling the loop up and underneath, then you may have to loosen the wrapped rope slightly.

Step 5: Trim the excess cord from the top of the knot and as close to the wrapped rope as possible.

Hanger String (HS)

This technique is used to tie a cord onto a wall hanging or plant hanger so that it can hang on a wall. It is made by tying identical knots on opposite sides of a wooden dowel, driftwood, metal ring or frame using one piece of rope. You will need a hot glue gun for this technique.

Step 1: Cut a piece of rope to the desired length. Attach a Reverse Lark's Head (RLH) knot to the dowel, leaving at least 13cm (5in) of cord hanging on the short end of the rope or the length specified in the project instructions.

Step 2: The long end of the rope becomes the Holding Cord (HC) and the short end becomes the Working Cord (WC). Tie a Reverse Double Half Hitch Knot (RDHH) onto the HC with the WC. Tighten the knot. Turn the RLH upside down on the dowel so that the cords are facing up.

Step 3: Move to the other end of the dowel. Take the loose end of the rope behind and then over the top of the dowel. Leave at least 13cm (5in) of the cut end of the rope to work with.

Continued from previous page

Hanger String (HS)

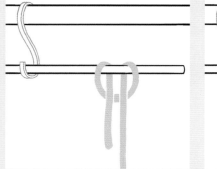

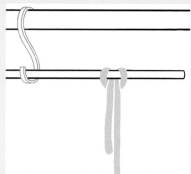

Step 4: Bring the short end of rope behind and across the long end of rope. Next bring it in front of the dowel and then up and over to the back of the dowel. Pull the cut end through the loop.

Step 5: Pull both hanging cords to tighten the knot. You have now made a second RLH.

Step 6: Repeat Step 2 and turn the dowel over so that you are looking at the back of it.

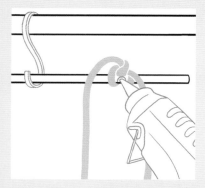

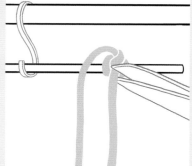

Step 7: Place a small dab of hot glue in between the two cords wrapped around the wooden dowel.

Step 8: Press the short end of cord down into the glue and hold it in place for a couple seconds. Be careful as the glue is very hot. Trim the short end of the cord off just below where it has been glued down.

Step 9: Repeat Steps 7–8 on the other end of the dowel.

KNOT AND TECHNIQUE LIBRARY

Techniques   Brushing

As you work your way through the projects in this book, you will come across instructions that direct you to brush out single strand string. This type of string is the easiest to brush out since it has lots of small threads that are loosely twisted together, making it easy for the comb or brush to pass through. It is best to start with one cord rather than attempting to brush out a few at a time so that you can see how easy it is going to be. With your comb or bristle brush, gently start to brush through a cord, starting at the very bottom and then gradually working your way up as the threads start to separate from one another. Most of the time the threads in single strand cotton string will brush out completely straight and will have a smooth and soft appearance. You may notice that some fluffy fibres accumulate at the bottom of the threads, which you can trim for clean and tidy ends.

If you are working with twisted or plied rope, you will first have to unravel the strands that have been wound together. Once all of the strands are hanging freely, you can brush them out in the same way as you would for single strand string. Since the strands in the rope were twisted, they may not fully straighten out after being brushed and they may have a wavy appearance.

When you are brushing out cords that are attached to your project it is important that you do it very gently and do not pull too much, as this could affect the overall design. I find that by holding the cord(s) that I am working on in one hand and then brushing with the other, I have full control of the tension that is being put on the cords and the project.

Trimming

Many people have told me that trimming their wall hanging is the most intimidating part of the entire process, since this will determine the final look of the project. For others, including myself, it is the most satisfying step because you finally get to see the finished product. There are a few different options when it comes to trimming your project, and as you complete the projects in this book, you will be able to decide which option is best for you.

Each of the projects in this book will provide measurements as well as the direction to trim the cords to reveal the final design. Before you start measuring or cutting, you should always tidy up the cords so that they are hanging or lying straight and check that they are all in order.

When it comes to trimming your finished project, be sure to take a step back and look at it from different angles before you make the final decision. You could even use pieces of tape to mock up the final trim for your wall hanging before you start cutting.

If you would like a perfectly angled and symmetrical cut, then I recommend that you measure each of the individual cords and carefully cut them at the specified length. You can save some time by measuring and trimming a number of cords at equal intervals along the entire row of cords, and then following the line of the cut cords to trim the remaining cords. This technique is faster but rarely achieves as perfect a cut as measuring each strand individually.

A trick I recently learned for trimming straight lines on larger projects with many cords is to measure the first and last cords in the row and then place a piece of tape across the cords, lining it up to the correct measurements from end to end. You can then trim along the tape with your shears or scissors. You can do this while your project is hanging vertically or lying down on a flat working surface. This would also work well with a rotary cutter.

If you have trimmed your project and you are not sure that you love the final result, try brushing out 2–3cm (1in or so) of the cut ends to add some extra texture and fullness in that area. Another option is to stagger the lengths of the cords by cutting every other cord a few centimetres (an inch or so) shorter. If you think that you may have accidentally cut the cords a little too short on a wall hanging, then you may be able to add an entirely new fringe with longer cords behind the cords that you trimmed too short. If you are working on your own design and you are not sure how to trim the cords, I recommend that you start by trimming off a small amount, step back and look at the project, and then decide if you want to keep going.

Fixing mistakes

Mistakes are going to occur regardless of your skill level, but rest assured that they are almost always fixable. In most situations, the easiest option is to simply untie the offending knots and start over. Always untie the knots gently and slowly to avoid snagging, particularly with single strand string, and to keep everything intact. Mistakes with braided cord or twisted rope are often easier to untie and resolve, as they are sturdy and hold their shape really well. I encourage you to take the extra time to double check your work as you move along through the instructions to avoid too many frustrating mistakes.

Unravelling

One of the simplest ways to add character and texture to a wall hanging or a plant hanger is to unravel the cords that you are working with. When I say 'unravel', I mean simply unwind or undo the obvious twist or spiral in the rope or string (see Essential terms, page 24). This will add additional texture and fullness to your piece. Unravelled cords can also be brushed out if desired.

If you are working with plied rope, then it will be easy to unravel the strings into separate bundles. I find that the easiest way to do this is to turn the bundle in the opposite direction to the twisted strands, starting from the top of the piece of rope and working down to the bottom, until you can see that all of the strands have started to detach from one another. Go ahead and remove one of the strands from the bundle. It may curl up and twist around itself and that is okay; leave it for now and return to the bundle, proceeding to remove one twisted strand at a time until they are all separated. Now you can smooth out the strands and let them hang freely and observe the beautiful texture that the unravelled rope brings to your project.

To unravel and separate single strand string, start off the same way as you did with the plied rope, by turning the string in the opposite direction to the twisted single strand. Start from the top of the string and gradually work your way to the bottom until you have what appears to be a straight bundle of strings or threads. At this point you can decide how many bundles that you would like to have, and you can start pulling out smaller bunches of threads, one by one. Once you have multiple smaller bundles, go ahead and smooth out each of the bundles so that they hang freely. The bundles should still have a slight twist to them, and you can clean them up by twisting the threads back in the direction that they were originally in.

How to prevent unravelling

Most of the time you will not want your rope or string to start unravelling while you are working on a project, since you will most likely need all of the rope intact in order to finish the design. Generally, you will only need to be concerned with twisted or plied rope, since it tends to unravel fairly easily – but sometimes single strand string may unravel a little bit, too.

My preferred method for holding rope or string together is to wrap a piece of tape tightly around the cut ends. Masking tape, magic or Scotch tape, packing tape, painter's tape and washi tape are all great options. Once you have completed the project, you can remove the tape with your hands or simply cut it off.

Other options for preventing unravelling include dipping the cut ends into melted wax and letting them dry; applying a small dab of hot glue and pinching the ends together; tying Overhand Knots at the bottom of each cord (see page 30); and tying small Gathering Knots with thread or yarn around the cut ends (see page 64).

Using steam

A garment steamer is an excellent tool for straightening out any ropes that have kinks in them. Kinks often happen on pieces of rope or string that have been stored or handled improperly and they are sometimes found at the end of a spool.

A garment steamer uses hot water steam to plump up fabric and to relax the fibres, eliminating kinks and other wrinkles. Most steamers have a base that contains a water reservoir and a heating element, a hose that carries the steam from the base to the nozzle, and a steam head or nozzle with a handle that releases channelled steam. Since these types of steamers have bendable hoses, they are perfect for using on macramé since you can easily move the light-weight steam head around to reach your entire project. You can also find small handheld garment steamers that will work nicely for your macramé projects.

Before you use steam on your projects, be aware that it will sometimes loosen up the twist of your string or rope a little bit. I find that this comes in handy for adding texture to the cut ends of cords. If you would like the cut ends to look slightly combed-out or frayed, you can apply steam to the ends and they will naturally unwind a little bit – this is a quick and easy way to finish off a project.

Be extra careful when you are using a garment steamer: the steam is extremely hot and can cause burns. Always read the manufacturer's safety guidelines and instructions before you attempt to use it on your projects.

Bundling long ropes

Keeping long pieces of rope tidy and free from knots can be a tricky task. Although there are a couple of tricks to keep a long rope manageable, you will still have to be attentive when you are working with each cord and do your best to keep everything tidy. One of the most frustrating things in macramé is having to start untangling long pieces of rope. Trust me when I say that it is always worth taking the extra time and care to avoid it.

My favourite method for bundling long strands of rope is quick and simple, and allows you to pull additional lengths instantly without having to untie your bundle. This way of bundling will only be useful when you are working with rope of a thin diameter, since you will be using your fingers to wind the bundle. This is also a good way to bundle and store longer pieces of rope that are no longer wrapped around the spool.

Begin by securing your rope to the dowel or driftwood (or as directed in the project). You will be bundling one cord at a time, so choose a cord to start with and make sure that there are no knots, tangles or twists.

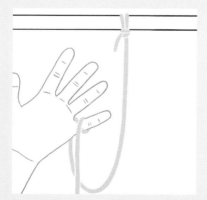

Step 1: Decide how much length of the rope you would like to keep outside of the bundle. Once decided, wrap the rope around your pinky finger.

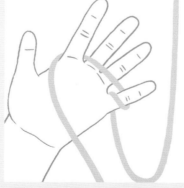

Step 2: With your palm facing up, bring the long end of the rope over and across your ring finger and middle finger, then under your index finger.

Step 3: Next, bring the same rope around your thumb moving from the palm side and then up and over the base of your thumb. Turn your hand over so you are now looking at the back of your hand.

KNOT AND TECHNIQUE LIBRARY

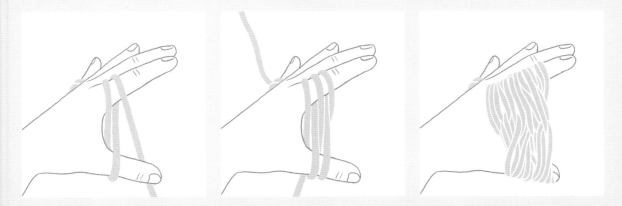

Step 4: Bring the rope under and over your index finger and then back under and over your thumb. Continue this step to make figures-of-eight with the rope until you reach the end.

Step 5: With your other hand, carefully slide the bundle off your fingers while holding onto the middle section. Hold the bundle firmly to keep the rope in position as you remove it.

Step 6: Wrap a rubber band around the centre of the bundle to hold it together.

You now have a tidy bundle of rope. To give yourself more rope to work with, simply pull on the rope coming out of the bundle that is also attached to the project. It should pull out easily and the bundle should hold its shape.

Projects

Mug rugs

YOU WILL NEED

Niroma Studio 3mm Single Twist
Cotton String:

13.5m (15yd) in Sage or Mustard
per mug rug

Sharp pair of scissors

Measuring tape or ruler

Fine-toothed comb

Optional: cork trivet and pins

SIZE

14.5cm (5¾in) diameter, including
a 2-cm (¾-in) fringe

KNOTS

Loop

Reverse Lark's Head (RLH)

Double Half Hitch (DHH)

Macramé mug rugs are a crowd favourite and also one of the easiest projects to make. These adorable round coasters are the perfect way to bring a little bohemian style into your home. Not only are they pretty, they're practical too, and will protect your furniture from a hot mug of tea or coffee. A four-pack could make a beautiful handmade gift that you can customize to suit any décor just by changing the colour of the string.

1. Cut one 152-cm (60-in) rope and five 86-cm (34-in) ropes in your chosen colour.

2. Make a Loop 8cm (3in) in diameter at one end of the 152-cm (60-in) rope, going in an anti-clockwise direction so that the long end is on the right, and then lay it down on a flat working surface. This rope becomes the Holding Cord (HC).

3. Fold one of the 86-cm (34-in) ropes in half and attach it to the Loop with a RLH where there are two pieces of cord overlapping. Tighten the RLH so that it is secure. Repeat with the four remaining ropes. These become the Working Cords (WCs).

4. Pull on the longer end of the HC while holding onto one of the RLHs to close the loop.

5. Lift the HC to the right (over the short end of the HC) and tie a DHH with the first WC to the right. The DHH should be as close to the row above it as possible. Repeat this step with the next WC to the right.

Project continues overleaf

Tip:
Once you have completed Steps 1–4, fasten the Reverse Lark's Head knots to a cork trivet with some pins. This will help to keep the cords in place as you turn the mug rug to complete the pattern.

PROJECTS

6. You should now have a gap between the DHH and the next WC to the right. Cut a rope that is twice the length of the cord to the left (for example, if the cord measures 25cm/10in, then cut a 50-cm/20-in rope). Fold the new rope in half and attach to the HC with a RLH to fill the gap. Moving in an anti-clockwise direction, continue with DHHs to make a spiral pattern and add rope as needed to fill any gaps. Each time a new rope is added, measure the cord to the left, cut a rope that is twice that measurement and attach to the HC with a RLH. When in doubt, add cords to ensure that the mug rug doesn't start to curve into a bowl shape. The DHHs should be tied gently and slightly loose, but tight enough to hold them in place directly below the row above.

7. Continue the pattern until the diameter reaches 10.5cm (4in). Tie the last DHH tightly.

8. Trim the cords to 2cm (¾in) and gently comb them out (see page 69). You may want to do additional trimming to tidy up the fringe after combing.

9. Turn the mug rug over and cut off the short end of the HC.

Keychain

Niroma Studio 3mm Single Twist
Cotton String:
   3.6m (4yd) in Sage, Mustard
   or Rose
Metal clasp with D-ring that has
   2cm (¾in) inner width
Sharp pair of scissors
Measuring tape or ruler
Optional: packing tape
Optional: cork trivet and pins

SIZE
17.5cm (7in), plus length of metal
   hardware

KNOTS
Lark's Head (LH)
Double Half Hitch (DHH)
Square (SQ)
Gathering Knot (GK)

These cute keychains are sure to catch everyone's attention, especially if you decide to make one in a bright, bold colour. Not only do they dress up your keys, but they can also accessorize your purse or favourite bag. This is a quick and easy project that requires very little string, making it a perfect starting point if you are new to macramé.

1. Cut three 108-cm (42½-in) ropes. Fold each rope in half and fasten to the D-ring with LHs.

2. C3 becomes the Holding Cord (HC). Tie DHHs onto the HC with C4–C6, moving from left to right to form a Downward Diagonal Line (DDL).

3. C3 becomes the HC. Tie DHHs onto the HC with C2–C1, moving from right to left to form a DDL.

4. Repeat Steps 2 and 3.

5. Tie a SQ with C2–C5.

6. C6 becomes the HC. Tie DHHs onto the HC with C5–C4, moving from right to left to form a DDL.

7. C1 becomes the HC. Tie DHHs onto the HC with C2–C4, moving from left to right to form a DDL.

8. Repeat Steps 6 and 7.

9. C4 becomes the HC. Tie DHHs onto the HC with C5–C6, moving from left to right to form a DDL.

10. Repeat Step 3.

11. Repeat Step 2.

12. Repeat Step 3.

13. Repeat Step 5.

14. Repeat Step 6.

15. Repeat Step 7.

Attach the metal clasp with D-ring to a cork trivet using pins or a clipboard to hold it in place. You can also use a piece of packing tape to secure the hardware to something to hold it still while you work on the pattern.

16. Repeat Step 6.

17. Repeat Step 7.

18. Turn the keychain over. Cut a 30-cm (12-in) rope and tie a 2-cm (¾-in) GK around the hanging cords.

19. Trim the hanging cords to 4.5cm (1¾in) below the GK.

Basic wall hanging

YOU WILL NEED

Mary Maker Studio 5mm Single
Twisted Cotton String:
  82m (90yd) in Rust
38cm (15in) wooden dowel
or driftwood with a 1.25–2.5-cm
  (½–1in-) diameter
Sharp pair of scissors
Measuring tape or ruler
Fine-toothed comb
Hot glue and glue gun
Optional: garment rail and S-hooks

SIZE

38 x 56cm (15 x 22in)
  (measurement does not include
  Hanger String)

KNOTS

Lark's Head (LH)
Square (SQ)
Alternating Square (ASQ)
Double Half Hitch (DHH)
Cord Alternating Square (CASQ)
Gathering Knot (GK)
Hanger String (HS)

Simple and stunning! This is one of the easier projects in the book because of its repetitive pattern. It also doesn't take very long to complete, especially if you are already comfortable tying Square knots. You can easily double or triple the length of this wall hanging by increasing the length of the dowel and by adding additional panels and sinnets.

1. Cut six 3.5-m (4-yd) ropes. Fold the ropes in half and secure them to the dowel with LHs. The ropes should be centred on the dowel.

2. Tie a row of SQs, starting with C1–C4. Tie a second row of ASQs. Repeat these steps until there are 38 rows of ASQs. Tie one SQ with C5–C8.

3. C12 becomes the Holding Cord (HC). Tie DHHs onto the HC with C11–C7, moving from right to left to form a Downward Diagonal Line (DDL). C1 becomes the HC. Tie DHHs onto the HC with C2–C7, moving from left to right to form a DDL. Repeat once more so that there are two sets of DDLs. Trim the hanging cords to 7.5cm (3in) from the knots above in a DDL and gently brush them out (see page 69). This completes the first, central panel.

4. Cut six more 3.5-m (4-yd) ropes. Fold the ropes in half and secure to the dowel with LHs 3.75-cm (1½in) to the left of the panel you just created. There should be a 3.75-cm (1½-in) space between the new ropes and the first panel you made. Repeat Steps 2 and 3.

5. Cut six more 3.5-m (4-yd) ropes. Fold the ropes in half and secure to the dowel with LHs, 3.75-cm (1½in) to the right of the first panel you created. There should be a 3.75-cm (1½-in) space between the new ropes and the first panel you made. Repeat Steps 2 and 3. You should now have three identical panels that are spaced 3.75-cm (1½in) apart.

Project continues overleaf

BASIC WALL HANGING

Tip:

If one of the panels ends up slightly shorter than the others, you can gently tug on it to add length.

6. Cut two 2.25-m (2½-yd) ropes. Fold the ropes in half and secure to the dowel with LHs in one of the 3.75-cm (1½-in) spaces between the panels. Tie four SQs, one above the other, to form a sinnet.

7. Measure down 3cm (1¼in) and tie a CASQ. Repeat two more times.

8. Tie three SQs.

9. Repeat Steps 7 and 8.

10. Measure down 3cm (1¼in) and tie a CASQ.

11. Cut one 30-cm (12-in) rope and use it to tie a 2.5-cm (1-in) GK below the last SQ. Trim the cords 7.5cm (3in) from the bottom of the GK and gently brush them out.

12. Repeat Steps 6–11 in the other 3.75-cm (1½-in) space between the panels.

13. Repeat Steps 6–11 on the outside of the left panel and then on the outside of the right panel.

14. Cut a 90-cm (36-in) rope and tie a HS on the outside of all the cords on the dowel.

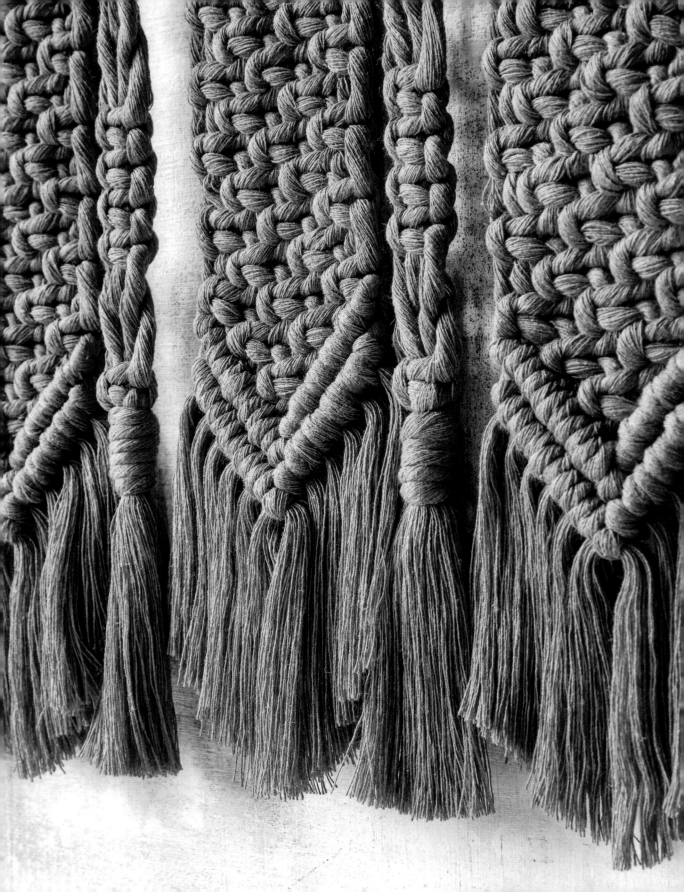

Plant rug

YOU WILL NEED

GANXXET 4mm Soft Cotton Single Strand Cord:

  45m (49yd) in Black, Dusty Rose or Navy Blue

Sharp pair of scissors

Measuring tape or ruler

Fine-toothed comb

Optional: cork trivet and pins

SIZE

30cm (132in) diameter, including a 3.75-cm (1½-in) fringe

KNOTS

Loop

Reverse Lark's Head (RLH)

Double Half Hitch (DHH)

With the rising popularity of house plants, it's no wonder that macramé plant rugs are a favourite. Not only are they attractive, they protect your furniture from water spills and surface scratches. Your plants will be happy to hang out on top of their own little rug and you can change the colour of string to match your décor. These circular mats are versatile and look gorgeous on coffee tables, underneath a bouquet of flowers, or placed under your favourite candles. You could even bring them into the kitchen or dining area and use them as trivets. Best of all, these adorable plant rugs will match your mug rugs perfectly.

1.   Cut one 5.5-m (6-yd) rope and five 1.7-m (2-yd) ropes.

2.   Make a Loop 8cm (3in) in diameter at one end of the 5.5-m (6-yd) rope, going in an anti-clockwise direction so that the long end is on the right, and lay it down on a flat working surface. This will become the Holding Cord (HC).

3.   Fold one 1.7-m (2-yd) rope in half and attach it to the Loop with a RLH where there are two cords overlapping. Tighten the RLH so that it is secure. Repeat with the four remaining ropes. These become Working Cords (WCs).

4.   Pull on the longer end of the HC while holding onto one of the RLH to close the loop.

5.   Lift the HC to the right (over the short end of the HC) and tie a DHH with the first WC to the right. The DHH should be as close to the row above it as possible. Repeat this step with the next WC to the right.

Project continues overleaf

Tip:

Once you have completed Steps 1–4, you can fasten the Reverse Lark's Head knots to a cork trivet with some pins. This will help to keep the cords in place as you turn the plant rug to complete the spiral pattern. Continue to add pins as you form the plant rug to secure it to the trivet.

PROJECTS

6. You should now have a gap between the DHH and the next WC to the right. Cut another 1.7-m (2-yd) rope, fold it in half and attach it to the HC with a RLH to fill the gap. Moving in an anti-clockwise direction, continue with DHHs to make a spiral pattern and add rope as needed to fill any gaps. Each time a new rope is added, measure the cord to the left, cut a rope that is twice that measurement and attach it to the HC with a RLH. When in doubt, add cords to ensure that the plant rug doesn't start to curve into a bowl shape.

7. Continue the pattern until the diameter reaches 22.5cm (9in). Tie the last DHH tightly.

8. Trim the cords to 3.75cm (1½in) long and gently comb them out (see page 69). You may want to do additional trimming to tidy up the fringe after it has been combed.

9. Turn the plant rug over and cut off the short end of the HC.

Basic plant hanger

YOU WILL NEED
Createaholic 5mm Cotton String:
   73m (80yd) in Vanilla (Natural)
   or Terracotta
Sharp pair of scissors
Measuring tape or ruler
Optional: garment rail and S-hook

SIZE
105cm (41½in) when empty

KNOTS
Square (SQ)
Gathering Knot (GK)
Alternating Squares (ASQ)

Isn't this one lovely? This simple contemporary design is bound to be a beautiful addition to your home and it's the perfect excuse to add another house plant to your collection. The pattern is repetitive, which makes this project an easy one for beginners. This macramé hanger looks best when holding a plant pot that's 10–15cm (4–6in) in diameter. Replace your potted plant with a glass terrarium to house your air plants, mini lights, or holiday décor as the seasons change.

1. Cut twelve 4.3-m (4¾-yd) ropes. Put the twelve ropes together and line up one set of the cut ends.

2. Cut one 2.7-m (3-yd) piece of rope and fold it in half to find the middle point. This rope becomes the Working Cord (WC). Measure 192cm (75½in) down from the cut ends on one side of the bundle and place the middle point of the WC behind the bundle. The twelve long ropes become Filler Cords (FCs). Use the WC to tie sixteen SQs around the FCs, starting at the 192-cm (75½-in) measurement and moving towards the middle point/opposite end of the bundle. This will form a sinnet in the middle of the FCs.

3. Fold the sinnet in half. Cut one 85-cm (33½-in) rope and tie a 3-cm (1¼-in) GK around all twenty-four cords. Trim the two leftover cords from the sinnet of SQs as close to the GK as possible, so that they are no longer visible. You should now have twenty-four cords hanging below the GK.

4. Pick up four cords and tie a SQ below the GK. Pick up four more cords – two on the left side of the SQ and two on the right side of the SQ. Tie two ASQs, using the four cords from the SQ in the first row and the four new cords to make a second row. Continue tying ASQs with the same eight cords to make forty rows. Repeat this step two more times to make three identical panels of ASQs.

Project continues overleaf

Tip:

Once you have reached Step 4, hang the top loop on a garment rail with an S-hook and then finish the project. This will help to keep the tension consistent and you can easily check to see that the panels and sinnets are lining up nicely. You may want to stand while working on the top part of the plant hanger and then sit on a chair once you reach the bottom part in order to keep your eyes in line with the section that you are working on.

5. Cut one 2.8-m (3-yd) rope and fold it in half to find the middle point. This rope becomes the WC. Place the middle point of the WC behind four cords hanging below one of the ASQs in a panel. The four hanging cords become FCs. Use the WC to tie twelve SQs around the FCs. Repeat this step five more times to create six sinnets of SQs.

6. Place two of the ASQ panels side by side so that four sinnets of SQs are also side by side. Pick up the second and third sinnets in the row of four. C1 and C12 become WCs and C2–C11 become FCs. Use the WCs to tie three SQs around the FCs. Repeat this step twice more to connect all of the panels together.

7. Cut one 85-cm (33½-in) rope and tie a 3-cm (1¼-in) GK around all of the cords, starting 8cm (3in) down from the last set of SQs. Ensure that the GK is tied tightly, as it will support the weight of the potted plant.

8. Trim all of the hanging cords 20cm (8in) below the GK (or leave them longer if you wish).

Mini wall hanging

YOU WILL NEED

Mary Maker Studio 5mm Single
Twisted Cotton String:
  32m (35yd) in Stone Grey
18.5cm (7¼in) wooden dowel or
  driftwood with a 1-cm (½-in)
  diameter
Sharp pair of scissors
Measuring tape or ruler
Fine-toothed comb
Hot glue and glue gun
Optional: garment rail and S-hooks
Optional: rotary cutter and cutting
  mat

SIZE

18.5 x 43cm (7¼ x 17in)
  (measurement does not include
  Hanger String)

KNOTS

Lark's Head (LH)
Square (SQ)
Alternating Square (ASQ)
Double Half Hitch (DHH)
Reverse Double Half Hitch (RDHH)
Hanger String (HS)

Sometimes all you need is a little wall hanging to decorate a small space. This one looks beautiful hanging on its own or as part of a gallery wall of photographs or a curated collection of art. The bottom fringe combs out effortlessly and looks fluffy and full once you're done. This could be a lovely handmade gift that you'd be proud to say you made yourself.

1. Cut twelve 2.6-m (3-yd) ropes. Fold the ropes in half and secure to the dowel with LHs. The ropes should be centred on the dowel.

2. Tie a row of SQs starting with C1–C4. For the second row, skip C1–C2 and tie a row of ASQs starting with C3–C6; skip C23–C24. Continue the pattern by tying decreasing ASQs to create an upside-down triangle.

3. C24 becomes the Holding Cord (HC). Tie DHHs onto the HC with C23–C13, moving from right to left to form a Downward Diagonal Line (DDL). C1 becomes the HC. Tie DHHs onto the HC with C2–C13, moving from left to right to form a DDL and to close the V-shape.

4. Drop down 2.5cm (1in) and repeat Step 3.

5. Make a DDL of SQs by tying SQs with C1–C4, C3–C6, C5–C8, C7–C10 and C9–C12. Create another DDL of SQs by tying SQs with C21–C24, C19–C22, C17–C20, C15–C18, C13–C16 and C11–C14.

6. Repeat Steps 3 and 4.

7. Tie a SQ with C1–C4, C3–C6, C1–C4, C21–C24, C19–C22 and C21–C24.

8. C19 becomes the HC. Tie DHHs onto the HC with C18–C13, moving from right to left to form a DDL. C6 becomes the HC. Tie DHHs onto the HC with C7–C13, moving from left to right to form a DDL and to close the V-shape.

Project continues overleaf

If you have a rotary cutter and cutting mat, you can get a really clean cut on the bottom fringe by using these tools. Once you have finished Step 14, lay the wall hanging down on the mat, line it up with the correct measurement and then cut the cords with the rotary cutter. After you have brushed out the fringe, you can clean up it up by cutting the ends one more time with your rotary cutter and mat.

9. C19 becomes the HC. Tie DHHs onto the HC with C20–C24, moving from left to right to form a DDL. C6 becomes the HC. Tie DHHs onto the HC with C5–C1, moving from right to left to form a DDL.

10. Tie SQs with C5–C8 and C17–C20. C9 becomes the HC. Tie DHHs onto the HC with C8–C7, moving from right to left to form a DDL. C16 becomes the HC. Tie DHHs onto the HC with C17–C18, moving from left to right to form a DDL. Tie SQs with C8–C11 and then with C14–C17. C13 becomes the HC. Tie DHHs onto the HC with C14–C15, moving from left to right to form a DDL. C12 becomes the HC. Tie DHHs onto the HC with C11–C10, moving from right to left to form a DDL. Tie a SQ with C11–C14.

11. C21 becomes the HC. Tie DHHs onto the HC with C20–C13, moving from right to left to form a DDL. C4 becomes the HC. Tie DHHs onto the HC with C5–C13, moving from left to right to form a DDL.

12. C22 becomes the HC. Tie RDHHs onto the HC with C21–C13, moving from right to left to form a DDL. C3 becomes the HC. Tie RDHHs onto the HC with C4–C13, moving from left to right to form a DDL.

13. C23 becomes the HC. Tie RDHHs onto the HC with C22–C13, moving from right to left to form a DDL. C2 becomes the HC. Tie RDHHs onto the HC with C3–C13, moving from left to right to form a DDL.

14. Repeat Steps 3 and 4.

15. Trim the cords 10cm (4in) from the DDL above and gently brush them out (see page 69).

16. Cut a 60-cm (24-in) rope and tie a HS on the outside of all the cords fastened to the dowel.

Yoga mat carrier

YOU WILL NEED
Createaholic 5mm Cotton String:
  16.8m (18½yd) in Mint
  10m (11yd) in Vanilla (Natural)
Sharp pair of scissors
Measuring tape or ruler
Optional: garment rail and S-hooks

SIZE
180cm (71in) long

KNOTS
Gathering Knot (GK)
Square (SQ)

This handy carrier will make carrying your mat to your next yoga class a breeze. You can sling it over your shoulder or hold it in your hand, as both options are equally comfortable. If yoga isn't your thing, you can use it to carry a rolled-up blanket to your next picnic in the park, or for your beach mat on your next holiday.

1. Cut two 6-m (6½-yd) ropes in Mint and two 5-m (5½-yd) ropes in Natural. Put the four ropes together and line up one set of the cut ends.

2. Cut one 2.1-m (2¼-yd) rope in Mint and use it to tie a 17-cm (6¾-in) GK that starts 15cm (6in) from the cut ends and wraps down towards the opposite end of the bundle. When finishing the GK, only pull up far enough to just hide the end under the wrapped rope, as it will be too difficult to pull it all the way through.

3. Fold the GK in half and hold the eight cords together. Cut a 60-cm (24-in) rope in Mint and tie a 3.5-cm (1½-in) GK below the folded GK.

4. Tie forty SQs below the GK, using the Natural cords as Filler Cords (FCs) and the Mint cords as Working Cords (WCs).

5. The WCs now become the FCs and the FCs become the WCs. Drop down 5cm (2in) and tie fifty-seven SQs.

Project continues overleaf

Tips:
Once you have finished Step 3, hang the folded Gathering Knot (GK) on a garment rail with an S-hook while you complete the sinnet. This will help to keep the tension consistent as you work on the project.

You may want to bundle the Working Cords (WCs) once you reach Step 5 to avoid tangling (see page 76).

6.   The WCs now become the FCs and the FCs become the WCs. Drop down 5cm (2in) and tie forty SQs.

7.   Cut one 2.1-m (2¼-yd) rope in Mint and use it to tie a 17-cm (6¾-in) GK that starts 3.5cm (1½in) down from the last SQ in the sinnet. When finishing the GK, only pull up far enough to just hide the end under the wrapped rope, as it will be too difficult to pull it all the way through.

8.   Repeat Step 3.

9.   Trim the hanging cords to match the other end of the strap.

10. Pull one of the looped ends through the other loop until you have a circle shape that is approximately the same size as a rolled-up yoga mat. Carefully pull the circle you just made, along with the loop, through the other loop on the opposite end to create another circle shape. You will now have a circle at each end of the strap in which to place your mat.

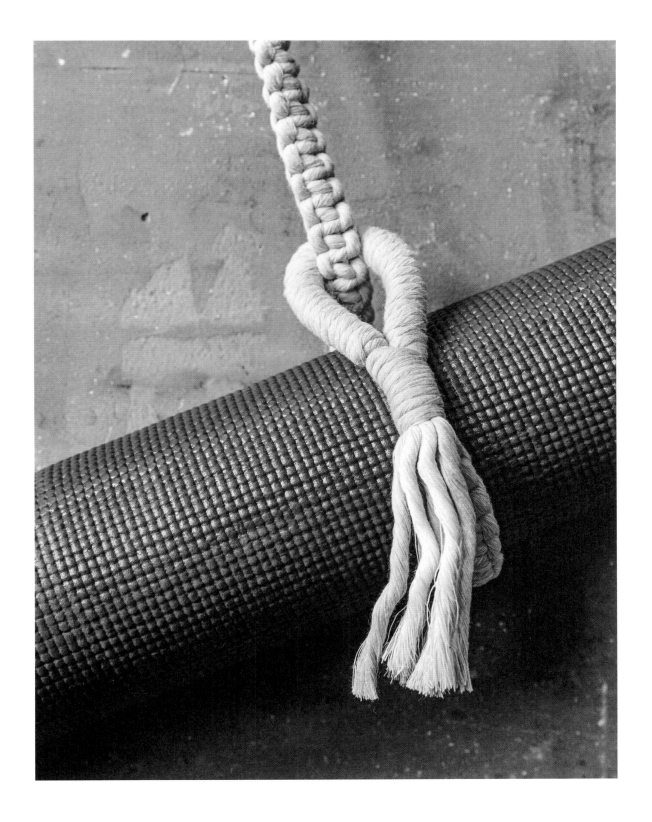

YOGA MAT CARRIER

Intermediate wall hanging

This wall hanging has lots of pretty little details and is the perfect piece for a modern boho-chic home. The gold rings pair beautifully with the soft, colourful string and they add just the right amount of shine. If the pink string is too bold for you, then consider using a neutral shade such as a natural unbleached cotton, warm grey or soft white.

1. Cut ten 2.7-m (3-yd) ropes. Fold the ropes in half and secure onto the 15-cm (6-in) ring with LHs. The LHs should be side by side at the top of the metal ring and the cut ends should hang down past the bottom of the ring.

2. Tie a row of SQs, starting with C1–C4. For the second row, skip C1–C2 and tie a row of ASQs starting with C3–C6 and skipping C19–C20. Continue the pattern by tying decreasing ASQs to make an upside-down triangle shape.

3. C20 becomes the Holding Cord (HC). Tie DHHs onto the HC with C19–C11, moving from right to left to form a Downward Diagonal Line (DDL). C1 becomes the HC. Tie DHHs onto the HC with C2–C11, moving from left to right to form a DDL and to close the V-shape.

4. C20 becomes the HC. Tie RDHHs onto the HC with C19–C11, moving from right to left to form a DDL. C1 becomes the HC. Tie RDHHs onto the HC with C2–C11, moving from left to right to form a DDL and to close the V-shape.

5. Repeat Step 3.

6. C18 becomes the HC. Tie DHHs onto the HC with C17–C11, moving from right to left to form a DDL. C3 becomes the HC. Tie DHHs onto the HC with C4–C11, moving from left to right to form a DDL and to close the V-shape.

Project continues overleaf

7. C16 becomes the HC. Tie DHHs onto the HC with C15–C11, moving from right to left to form a DDL. C5 becomes the HC. Tie DHHs onto the HC with C6–C11, moving from left to right to form a DDL and to close the V-shape.

8. C14 becomes the HC. Tie DHHs onto the HC with C13–C11, moving from right to left to form a DDL. C7 becomes the HC. Tie DHHs onto the HC with C8–C11, moving from left to right to form a DDL and to close the V-shape.

9. Move the cords so that they hang behind the bottom of the ring. Tie the cords to the bottom centre of the ring with DHHs, starting with C10 and C11 (middle cords), and then with C9 and C12. Continue attaching the cords to the ring, working from the innermost cords to the outermost cords until they're all fastened to the ring.

10. Repeat Steps 2 and 3.

11. C2 becomes the HC. Tie DHHs onto the HC with C3–C4, moving from left to right to form a DDL. C2 becomes the HC. Tie a DHH onto the HC with C1, moving from right to left to form a DDL. C4 becomes the HC. Tie a DHH onto the HC with C3, moving from right to left to form a DDL. C1 becomes the HC. Tie a DHH onto the HC with C2, moving from left to right to form a DDL. Repeat five more times. C2 becomes the HC. Tie a DHH onto the HC with C3.

12. C18 becomes the HC. Tie DHHs onto the HC with C19–C20, moving from left to right to form a DDL. C18 becomes the HC. Tie a DHH onto the HC with C17m moving from right to left to form a DDL. C20 becomes the HC. Tie a DHH onto the HC with C19, moving from right to left to form a DDL. C17 becomes the HC. Tie a DHH onto the HC with C18, moving from left to right to form a DDL. Repeat five more times. C18 becomes the HC. Tie a DHH onto the HC with C19.

13. C11 becomes the HC. Tie a DHH onto the HC with C12, moving from left to right to form a DDL. C10 becomes the HC. Tie a DHH onto the HC with C9, moving from right to left to form a DDL. C12 becomes the HC. Tie a DHH onto the HC with C11, moving from right to left to form a DDL. C9 becomes the HC. Tie DHHs onto the HC with C10–C11, moving from left to right to form a DDL. Repeat five more times.

14. Tie a SQ with C5–C8, measure 1.5cm (½in) down and tie a CASQ, and then repeat three more times. Tie a SQ with C13–C16, measure 1.5cm (½in) down and tie a CASQ, and then repeat three more times.

15. Cut five 30-cm (12-in) ropes and tie 2-cm (¾-in) GKs around C1–C4, C5–C8, C9–C12, C13–C16 and C17–C20. Trim the cords 7cm (2¾in) below the GK and gently brush them out (see page 69).

16. Cut twenty-four 72-cm (28¼-in) ropes. Fold the ropes in half and secure to the bottom of the 20-cm (8-in) ring with RLHs. The cords should be side by side at the bottom of the metal ring. Gently brush out 3cm (1¼in) of the cut ends of the cords.

17. Cut one 25-cm (10-in) rope. Fold the rope in half and tie an OLK 2cm (¾in) down from the cut ends. Slip the OLK through the middle SQ at the top of the 15-cm (6-in) ring and tie a LH around both rings to hold them together and to hang the wall hanging. The cords on the 20-cm (8-in) ring should be centred behind the pattern on the 15-cm (6-in) ring. The cords on the 15-cm (6-in) ring should be in front of the cords on the 20-cm (8-in) ring.

Wall hanging with pot

YOU WILL NEED
GANXXET 4mm Soft Cotton Single
Strand Cord:
   63m (69yd) in Camel
22.5cm (9in) wooden dowel or
   driftwood with a 1.5–2-cm
   (½–¾-in) diameter
10–12cm (4–4¾in) plant pot
Sharp pair of scissors
Measuring tape or ruler
Hot glue and glue gun
Optional: garment rail and S-hooks

SIZE
22.5 x 78cm (9 x 31in)
   (measurement does not include
   Hanger String)

KNOTS
Lark's Head (LH)
Square (SQ)
Alternating Square (ASQ)
Double Half Hitch (DHH)
Reverse Double Half Hitch (RDHH)
Gathering Knot (GK)
Hanger String (HS)

Tip:
If you want to hang this outside in
your garden or patio, replace the
recommended cotton string with
weather-resistant polyester or
nylon rope.

Give life to your walls (literally) with this stylish wall hanging that doubles as a plant holder. This design hangs flat against the wall and holds a standard 10–12cm (4–4¾in) pot. I personally love how this plant holder looks when paired with a cascading golden pothos or a heart-leaf philodendron that fills the wall below it. A matching pair looks stunning above bedside tables or on either side of a window.

1. Cut sixteen 3.8-m (4-yd) ropes. Fold the ropes in half and secure to the dowel or driftwood with LHs. The ropes should be centred on the dowel or driftwood.

2. Tie a row of SQs starting with C1–C4. For the second row, skip C1–C2 and tie a row of ASQs, starting with C3–C6 and skipping C31–C32. Continue the pattern by tying decreasing ASQs to make an upside-down triangle shape. There should be a total of eight rows.

3. C32 becomes the Holding Cord (HC). Tie DHHs onto the HC with C31–C17, moving from right to left to form a Downward Diagonal Line (DDL). C1 becomes the HC. Tie DHHs onto the HC with C2–C17, moving from left to right to form a DDL and to close the V-shape.

4. C32 becomes the HC. Tie RDHHs onto the HC with C31–C17, moving from right to left to form a DDL. C1 becomes the HC. Tie RDHHs onto the HC with C2–C17, moving from left to right to form a DDL and to close the V-shape. Repeat this step once more.

5. Repeat Step 3.

6. Tie a SQ with C1–C4, C2–C5, C1–C4, C29–C32, C27–C30 and C29–C32.

7. C7 becomes the HC. Tie DHHs onto the HC with C6–C1, moving from right to left to form a DDL. C8 becomes the HC. Tie DHHs onto the HC with C7–C1, moving from right to left to form a DDL. C26 becomes the HC. Tie DHHs onto the HC with C27–C32, moving from left to right to form a DDL. C25 becomes the HC. Tie DHHs onto the HC with C26–C32, moving from left to right to form a DDL.

Project continues overleaf

8. Tie a SQ with C7–C10, C5–C8, C3–C6, C1–C4, C9–C12, C7–C10, C5–C8, C3–C6, C1–C4, C11–C14, C9–C12, C7–C10, C5–C8, C3–C6 and C1–C4.

9. Tie a SQ with C23–C26, C25–C28, C27–C30, C29–C32, C21–C24, C23–C26, C25–C28, C27–C30, C29–C32, C19–C22, C21–C24, C23–C26, C25–C28, C27–C30 and C29–C32.

10. C18 becomes the HC. Tie DHHs onto the HC with C19–C32, moving from left to right to form a DDL. C15 becomes the HC. Tie DHHs onto the HC with C14–C1, moving from right to left to form a DDL. C17 becomes the HC. Tie DHHs onto the HC with C18–C32, moving from left to right to form a DDL. C16 becomes the HC. Tie DHHs onto the HC with C15–C1, moving from right to left to form a DDL.

11. Tie a SQ with C15–C18. Continue tying increasing ASQs to make eight rows. For the ninth row, continue the pattern with decreasing ASQs to finish the bottom half of the diamond shape. There should be fifteen rows of ASQs.

12. Repeat Step 3 twice.

13. Pick up C1, C2, C31 and C32, measure down 26cm (10¼in) and tie a SQ using C1 and C32 as Filler Cords (FCs) and C2 and C31 as Working Cords (WCs). Start a second row of ASQs with C3, C4 and the two cords on the left side of the SQ you just tied (C3 and the left cord below the SQ will be FCs). In the same row, make another ASQ using C29, C30 and the two cords on the right side of the first SQ you tied (C30 and the right cord below the first SQ will be FCs). Start a third row by making an ASQ with C5, C6 and the two cords on the left side of the first ASQ in the second row (C5 and the left cord below the first ASQ in the second row will be the FCs). In the same row, make another ASQ using C27, C28 and the two cords on the right side of the second ASQ in the second row (C28 and the right cord below the second ASQ above will be the FCs). Tie an ASQ in the middle of the two ASQs in the third row to make a triangle shape. Tie two more decreasing rows of ASQs to finish the diamond shape.

14. Cut one 80-cm (32-in) rope for the GK. Hold your plant pot inside the cords to find the desired position. Gather all cords into one hand to determine where to tie a GK – I prefer to start the GK 2.5cm (1in) below the bottom tip of the diamond shape of ASQs, but it will depend on the shape and size of your pot. Tie a 3cm (1¼in) GK around all cords and put the pot in place. You can adjust any loose cords by gently pulling on the cords below the GK.

15. Trim the cords 20cm (8in) below the GK.

16. Cut one 75-cm (30-in) rope and tie a HS onto the wooden dowel or driftwood on the outside of all the cords fastened to the dowel.

Hanging ornament

YOU WILL NEED

Rope Shop 2.6mm Single Strand
Cotton:

   12.6m (14yd) in Natural per
   ornament

5-cm (2-in) wooden cabone ring
   (one per ornament)

Sharp pair of scissors

Measuring tape or ruler

Fine-toothed comb

Optional: cork trivet and pins

SIZE

16cm (6¼in) diameter
   (measurement does not include
   Hanger String)

KNOTS

Reverse Lark's Head (RLH)

Double Half Hitch (DHH)

Overhand Loop Knot (OLK)

Use these adorable macramé snowflakes to decorate your home for the holidays. They hang beautifully from a tree branch and the natural string is stunning against the deep green needles of a pine or spruce tree. Make five or more and tie them onto a piece of string to make a holiday bunting that you could hang under a mantel or across a window.

1. Cut two 76-cm (30-in) ropes and nineteen 58-cm (23-in) ropes.

2. Fold one 76-cm (30-in) rope and two 58-cm (23-in) ropes in half and attach to the cabone ring with RLHs. The long rope should be in the middle of the two shorter ropes.

3. C1 becomes the Holding Cord (HC). Tie DHHs onto the HC with C2–C3, moving from left to right to form a Downward Diagonal Line (DDL). C6 becomes the HC. Tie DHHs onto the HC with C5–C4, moving from right to left to form a DDL and to close the V-shape.

4. Repeat Steps 2 and 3 one more time. The second V-shape of DHHs should be directly beside the first V-shape of DHHs and to the right.

Project continues overleaf

PROJECTS

Rope Shop measures the thickness of their string when it is pulled tightly. Most other brands measure the thickness of their string when it is relaxed; therefore, if you are using loosely wound string, I recommend that you purchase 3mm single twisted string for this project. You may find it helpful to attach the ornament to a cork trivet with pins to hold it in place as you work on the project.

5. Repeat Steps 2 and 3 five more times with the remaining 58-cm (23-in) ropes to continue the pattern.

6. Gather six of the cords in between two of the V-shapes of DHHs and set the remaining cords aside to be worked on later. C6 becomes the HC. Tie DHHs onto the HC with C5–C4, moving from right to left to form a DDL. C1 becomes the HC. Tie DHHs onto the HC with C2–C4, moving from left to right to form a DDL and to close the V-shape. Repeat this step once more to make two V-shapes of DHHs, one directly below the other.

7. Repeat Step 6 six more times to continue the pattern around the ornament.

8. Find the two longest cords coming from the bottom point of one of the V-shapes. Tie an OLK using both cords 5cm (2in) above the point of the V-shape. Trim the cut ends to 6mm (¼in) above the OLK to complete the Hanger String.

9. Trim the remaining nineteen cords to 1cm (½in) and gently brush out the fringe (see page 69).

Bath mat

YOU WILL NEED

Createaholic 5mm Cotton String:
  204m (223yd) in Vanilla (Natural)
Sharp pair of scissors
Measuring tape or ruler
Garment rail or dowel
Optional: painter's tape

SIZE

42.5 x 80cm (16¾ x 31½in)

KNOTS

Lark's Head (LH)
Alternating Square (ASQ)

Step out of your long relaxing bath and onto this soft and luxurious bath mat. This pretty design is made with natural cotton string that feels good under the feet and it lies flat, so is comfortable to stand on. This project is time-consuming, but it is very easy to do. Once you've attached the ropes onto a garment rail, you'll only be required to tie one type of knot. You can easily replace the recommended cotton string with jute rope to make a durable mat for your entryway.

1. Cut thirty-four 6-m (6½-yd) ropes. Fold each rope in half and attach to a garment rail or a 2.5-cm (1-in) diameter supporting dowel with LHs.

2. Measure down 4cm (1½in) and tie nine rows of ASQs.

3. Measure down 3.5cm (1¼in) and tie five rows of ASQs.

4. Measure down 3.5cm (1¼in) and tie three rows of ASQs.

5. Repeat Step 3.

6. Repeat Step 4.

7. Repeat Step 3.

8. Measure down 3.5cm (1¼in) and tie nine rows of ASQs.

9. Remove the mat from the garment rail or supporting dowel by cutting through the middle of the LHs.

10. Trim the cords on both ends of the mat to 7.5cm (3in) to create a fringe.

Tip:
To keep the section between the Alternating Squares uniform, you can use painter's tape to help with spacing. Cut a piece of tape long enough to go across your rows and press the sticky side of the tape against your clothing a couple of times to remove most of the stickiness. Gently attach it to the back of the cords to keep an even space of 3.5cm (1¼in) between sections.

Double plant hanger

YOU WILL NEED

Createaholic 4mm 3-ply Cotton
Rope:
   39.2m (42.9yd) in Fiord Blue
Sharp pair of scissors
Measuring tape or ruler
Masking tape
Optional: garment rail and S-hook
Optional: six 2.5-cm (1-in) wooden
beads with large holes

SIZE
145cm (57in) when empty

KNOTS
Square (SQ)
Gathering Knot (GK)
Left Facing Half Square (LHSQ)
Alternating Square (ASQ)

What's better than a plant hanger? A double plant hanger! With only four types of knots, this impressive project will hold two of your favourite potted plants. You'll want to hang this one from the ceiling or from a curtain rod if you have tall windows, because it's rather long. If you'd like to shorten the length, you can do so by reducing the number of Half Squares in the top and bottom sinnets. This plant hanger works best with 10–15-cm (4–6-in) pots.

1. Cut six 5.8-m (6¼-yd) ropes. Wrap each of the cut ends with a small piece of masking tape to prevent the rope from unravelling. Put the six ropes together and line up one set of the cut ends.

2. Cut one 2.3-m (2½-yd) rope. Wrap the cut ends with a small piece of masking tape to prevent the rope from unravelling. This rope becomes the Working Cord (WC). Fold the WC in half to find the middle point. Measure 2.8m (3yd) down from the cut ends on one side of the bundle and place the middle point of the WC behind the bundle. The six ropes in the bundle become Filler Cords (FCs). Use the WC to tie sixteen SQs around the FCs, starting at the 2.8-m (3-yd) measurement and moving down towards the middle point/opposite end of the bundle. This will make a sinnet in the middle of the cords.

3. Fold the sinnet in half. Cut one 70-cm (27½-in) rope and tie a 3-cm (1¼-in) GK around all twelve cords. Trim the two leftover cords from the sinnet of SQs as close to the GK as possible so that they are no longer visible. You will now have twelve cords hanging below the GK.

4. Pick up four cords below the GK and tie thirty-five LHSQs. Repeat this step two more times to make three matching sinnets of LHSQs.

Project continues overleaf

Once you have reached Step 4, hang the top loop of the plant hanger on a garment rail with an S-hook and then finish the project. This will help to keep the tension consistent and you can easily check to see that the sinnets are lining up nicely. You may want to stand while working on the top part of the plant hanger and then sit on a chair or floor once you reach the bottom part in order to keep your eyes in line with the section that you are working on.

5. Drop down 2cm (¾in) and tie a SQ. If using beads, thread the two FCs through one of the beads and then slide the bead up to the bottom of the SQ. Tie a SQ directly below the bead to hold it in place. Drop down 2cm (¾in) and tie a SQ. Repeat this step for the other two sinnets. If you are not using beads, drop down 2cm (¾in) and tie a SQ, then repeat once more. Repeat this step for the other two sinnets.

6. Place two of the sinnets side by side so that the two bottom SQs line up. Measure down 12cm (4¾in) and tie one ASQ with the hanging cords from both sinnets to join them together. Repeat this step two more times to connect all of the sinnets together.

7. Measure down 10cm (4in) and tie one ASQ with the hanging cords from the last set of SQs to join them together. Repeat this step two more times.

8. Cut one 70-cm (27½-in) rope and tie a 3-cm (1¼-in) GK around all twelve cords.

9. You will now have six long cords and six short cords hanging below the GK. Using two short cords as FCs and two long cords as WCs, tie fifty LHSQs. Repeat two more times to make three identical sinnets.

10. Repeat Steps 5, 6, 7 and 8.

11. Trim the cords 20cm (8in) below the bottom of the GK or leave them longer if you wish.

Advanced wall hanging

YOU WILL NEED

Niroma Studio 5mm Single Twist
Cotton String:

  70m (76½yd) in Antique Peach

27cm (10½in) wooden dowel or
  driftwood with a 1.5–2.5-cm
  (½–1-in) diameter

Sharp pair of scissors

Measuring tape or ruler

Fine-toothed comb

Hot glue and glue gun

Optional: garment rail and S-hooks

Optional: rubber bands

SIZE

27 x 68cm (10½ x 26¾in)
  (measurement does not include
  Hanger String)

KNOTS

Lark's Head (LH)

Square (SQ)

Double Half Hitch (DHH)

Alternating Square (ASQ)

Hanger String (HS)

This contemporary wall hanging is one of my favourites and will complement almost any style of home décor with its clean lines and modern look. This design might look complicated, but it's actually fairly simple to do and uses only a few different knots. The pattern repeats itself and once you get going, you'll be finishing up the diagonal lines in no time. Your friends will be impressed when you tell them that you made this one yourself!

1.   Cut eighteen 3.8-m (4¼-yd) ropes. Fold the ropes in half and attach to the wooden dowel with LHs. The LHs should be centred on the dowel.

2.   Tie one row of SQs, starting with C1–C4.

3.   C6 becomes the Holding Cord (HC). Tie DHHs onto the HC with C7–C12, moving from left to right to form a Downward Diagonal Line (DDL). Repeat the pattern using C18 as the HC and C19–C24 as the Working Cords (WCs). Repeat the pattern using C30 as the HC and C30–C36 as the WCs.

4.   C6 becomes the HC. Tie DHHs onto the HC with C5–C1, moving from right to left to form a DDL. Repeat the pattern using C18 as the HC and C17–C13 as the WCs. Repeat the pattern using C30 as the HC and C29–C25 as the WCs.

5.   C13 becomes the HC. Tie a DHH onto the HC, moving from right to left with C12. C25 becomes the HC. Tie a DHH onto the HC, moving from right to left with C24.

6.   Repeat Steps 3, 4 and 5 twice more to create three rows of zigzag lines.

Project continues overleaf

7. Using C2 and C11 as WCs, tie a SQ around Filler Cords (FCs) C3–C10. Using C14 and C23 as WCs, tie a SQ around FCs C15–C22. Using WCs C26 and C35, tie a SQ around FCs C27–C34.

8. C1 becomes the HC. Tie DHHs onto the HC with C2–C6, moving from left to right to form a DDL. Repeat the pattern using C13 as the HC and C14–C18 as the WCs. Repeat the pattern using C25 as the HC and C26–C30 as the WCs.

9. C12 becomes the HC. Tie DHHs onto the HC with C11–C7, moving from right to left to form a DDL. Repeat the pattern using C24 as the HC and C23–C19 as the WCs. Repeat the pattern using C36 as the HC and C35–C31 as the WCs.

10. C6 becomes the HC. Tie a DHH onto the HC, moving from left to right with C7. C18 becomes the HC. Tie a DHH onto the HC, moving from left to right with C19. C30 becomes the HC. Tie a DHH onto the HC, moving from left to right with C31.

11. C13 becomes the HC. Tie DHHs onto the HC with C12–C7, moving from right to left to form a DDL. Repeat the pattern using C25 as the HC and C24–C19 as the WCs. Repeat the pattern using C36 as the HC and C35–C31 as the WCs.

12. C1 becomes the HC. Tie DHHs onto the HC with C2–C7, moving from left to right to form a DDL. Repeat the pattern using C13 as the HC and C14–C19 as the WCs. Repeat the pattern using C25 as the HC and C26–C31 as the WCs.

13. Repeat Steps 11 and 12.

14. Using WCs C8 and C17, tie a SQ around FCs C9–C16. Using WCs C20 and C29, tie a SQ around FCs C21–C28. Using WCs C1 and C5, tie a SQ around FCs C2–C4. Using WCs C32 and C36, tie a SQ around FCs C33–C35. All four SQs should be in a straight horizontal line with the bottom points of the V-shapes.

15. C7 becomes the HC. Tie DHHs onto the HC with C8–C12, moving from left to right to form a DDL. Repeat the pattern using C19 as the HC and C20–C24 as the WCs. Repeat the pattern using C31 as the HC and C32–C36 as the WCs.

16. Repeat Steps 4, 5, 6, 7, 8, 9 and 10.

17. Repeat Steps 11 and 12 twice more to repeat the pattern and to create three rows of zigzag lines.

18. Tie ASQs with C11–C14, C9–C12, C13–C16, C7–C10, C11–C14, C15–C18, C9–C12, C13–C16 and C11–C14.

19. Tie ASQs with C23–C26, C21–C24, C25–C28, C19–C22, C23–C26, C27–C30, C21–C24, C25–C28 and C23–C26.

20. Tie ASQs with C1–C4, C3–C6, C1–C4, C33–C36, C31–C34 and C33–C36.

21. Tie a SQ with C5–C8, 5cm (2in) down from the V-shape above. Repeat with C17–C20 and C29–C32.

22. Tie a SQ with C1–C4, 7.5cm (3in) down from the SQ above. Repeat with C11–C14, C23–C26 and C33–C36.

23. Tie a SQ with C5–C8, 7.5cm (3in) down from the V-shape above. Repeat with C17–C20 and C29–C32.

24. Measure 68cm (27¾in) down from the top of the wooden dowel and trim the hanging cords. You can leave the ends in a straight horizontal line or stagger the lengths by cutting some cords a little shorter than 68cm (27¾in). Gently comb out 2.5cm (1in) of the cut ends (see page 69).

25. Cut a 96-cm (40-in) rope and tie a HS on the outside of all the cords on the dowel.

PROJECTS

Market bag

YOU WILL NEED
<u>GANXXET 2mm 3-Ply Cotton</u>
<u>Rope:</u>
  116.5m (127½ yd) in Soft Blue
Sharp pair of scissors
Measuring tape or ruler
Masking tape
<u>Optional:</u> S-hook and garment rail
<u>Optional:</u> sewing needle and thread
  in colour to match rope

SIZE
27.5 x 77.5cm (11 x 30½in)
  when flat

KNOTS
Square (SQ)
Gathering Knot (GK)
Overhand Knot (OK)
Alternating Squares (ASQ)

This versatile shoulder bag is one of the most practical projects in this book and it serves a great purpose. Stop using single-use shopping bags and opt instead for your own handmade bag that you'll have for many years. Use it to carry fresh fruits and vegetables from your local market or freshly baked bread from your neighbourhood bakery. You could even use it to carry your towel, flip-flips and a book when you go to the beach. The handles are thick, sturdy and comfortable to wear over the shoulder.

1. Cut forty 2.6-m (2¾-yd) ropes and divide them into two bundles of twenty. Wrap each of the cut ends with a small piece of masking tape to prevent the rope from unravelling. Fold each of the bundles in half and line up the cut ends.

2. Cut one 4.6-m (5-yd) rope and fold it in half to find the middle point. This rope becomes the Working Cord (WC). Measure 115cm (45¼in) from the cut ends of one bundle. Place the middle point of the WC behind the bundle at 115cm (45¼in) and tie a tight SQ around the twenty cords, which now become Filler Cords (FCs).

3. Tie thirty-two SQs around the FCs, working your way back towards the middle point/opposite end of the bundle. This sinnet will make one of the handles for your bag.

4. Cut two 85-cm (33½-in) ropes and tie 4-cm (1½-in) GKs at both ends of the sinnet. Trim the two end cords from Step 3 as close to the GK as possible so that they aren't visible.

5. Repeat Steps 2, 3 and 4 with the other bundle of ropes. You will now have two identical pieces. Set one aside to be worked on later.

Project continues overleaf

6. Fold one of the handles in half and hang it over an S-hook on your garment rail. You can do this next part on a flat working surface if you prefer, but I find it easier to work on it while it's hanging from a hook.

7. Make a row of five SQs 15cm (6in) below the GKs. Make a second row of four ASQs 2cm (¾in) below the first row of SQs. Repeat with the cords hanging from the other side of the handle.

8. Connect both sides of the handle with a SQ 2cm (¾in) below the first row of SQs. This SQ will end up in the middle of the second row and will be made with the extra cords from the first row.

9. Repeat Steps 6, 7 and 8 with the other piece that you set aside.

10. Connect both pieces of the bag with a SQ 2cm (¾in) below the first row of SQs with the extra cords from the first row. Repeat on the other side, connecting both pieces and forming the opening of the bag.

11. Tie fifteen rows of ASQs, leaving 2cm (¾in) between each row.

12. Tie a sixteenth row of ASQs directly below the fifteenth row.

13. Lay the bag down on a flat surface. Place the handles one on top of the other and then line up the bottom row of SQs so that one is on top of the other.

14. To close the bottom of the bag, tie two OKs (one on top of the other) with a WC and FC from the SQ at the top far left and a WC and FC from the SQ at the bottom far left. Tie two more OKs with the other WC and FC from the SQ at the top far left and the other WC and FC from the SQ at the bottom far left. Continue the pattern by tying OKs across the bottom of the bag to close it. The knots should be tied tightly so that they don't come undone.

15. Trim the cords 6cm (2½in) below the OKs – or keep them longer if you prefer.

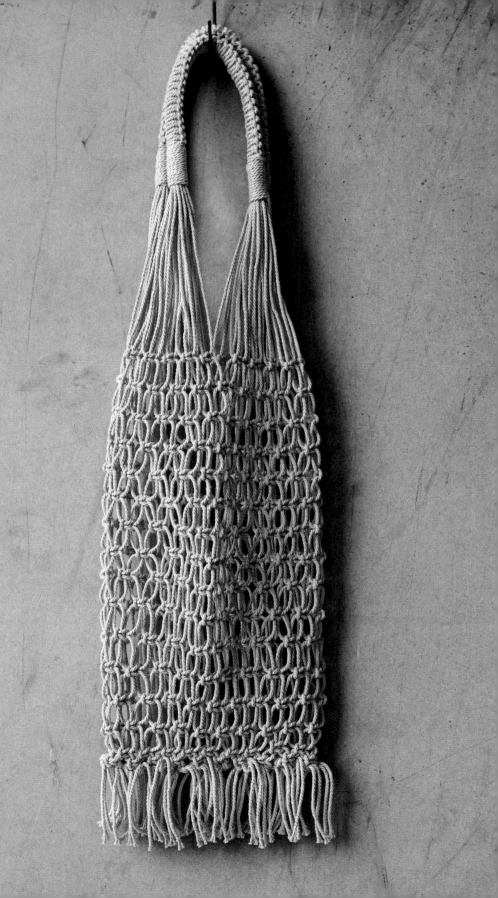

Lamp shade

YOU WILL NEED

Rope Shop 3.35mm Single Strand
Cotton Rope:
   238m (260yd) in Natural
Sharp pair of scissors
Measuring tape or ruler
Round lamp shade frame
   (top diameter 38cm/15in, bottom
   diameter 40cm/16in, height
   25cm/10in)
Hot glue and glue gun
Optional: S-hook and garment rail
Optional: sewing needle and thread
   in colour to match rope

SIZE

Top diameter 38.5cm (15¼in),
   bottom diameter 49cm (19¼in),
   height 35cm (13¾in)

KNOTS

RLH (Reverse Lark's Head)
ASQ (Alternating Square)
CASQ (Cord Alternating Square)
Berry Knot (BK)

Create an inviting glow and comforting ambience with this unique macramé lamp shade. The pattern allows the perfect amount of light to shine through and casts beautiful shadows around it. You can pair this lamp shade with a warm-white LED bulb or perhaps you'd prefer an LED Edison bulb instead. Whichever option you choose, ensure that your bulb won't get too hot and that you are lighting the space safely. The best part about this project is that it can be adapted to fit any size of frame, as long as you attach an even number of ropes in Step 1.

SETUP

You will need to suspend the top piece of the frame in order to work on the pattern. Cut a rope for each of the frame's spokes, long enough to hang the frame to a desired height from an S-hook on a garment rail (at least 60cm/24in per rope), centring each rope below the spokes and gathering all of the cut ends into one bundle. Then tie an Overhand Loop Knot (OLK) with all cords centred above the middle of the frame, so that it hangs level. Hang the OLK from an S-hook on a garment rail.

Alternatively, you can fasten the top piece of the frame to your lamp base in order to work on the pattern.

1.   Cut 116 2-m (2¼-yd) lengths of rope. Fold the ropes in half and secure to the top of the lamp shade frame with RLHs going all the way around the frame. The RLHs should sit side by side and should not be packed on too tightly.

2.   Tie three rows of ASQs.

3.   Drop down 3.5cm (1¼in) and tie a row of CASQs.

Project continues overleaf

Tip:
If you have a standard lamp shade, you can remove/detach the shade and use only the frame for this project.

4. Tie four rows of ASQs.

5. Repeat Step 3.

6. Tie two rows of ASQs.

7. Repeat Step 3.

8. Tie one row of BKs.

9. Tie one row of ASQs.

10. Trim the cords 7cm (2¾in) below the last row of SQs. If desired, trim some of the cords 1–2cm (½–¾in) shorter than the others to stagger the lengths.

11. Cut one 6-m (6½-yd) rope. Place a dab of hot glue on the bottom ring of the lamp shade frame to secure one end of the rope to the ring. Bundle the rope to prevent tangling (see page 76). Wrap the rope around the ring to cover the hardware completely. Once the ring is completely wrapped in rope, secure the end with a dab of hot glue. Trim off any excess cord.

12. Secure the rope-covered ring to the inside of the lamp shade so that it sits snugly inside. You can do this by using small dabs of hot glue to hold both pieces together or by hand-sewing the rope-covered ring onto the lamp shade with matching thread.

Tip:
Rope Shop measures the thickness of their string when it is pulled tightly. Most other brands measure the thickness of their string when it is relaxed; therefore, if you are using loosely wound string, I recommend that you purchase 4mm single twisted string for this project.

Fringed plant hanger

YOU WILL NEED

Niroma Studio 5mm Single Twisted
Cotton String:
   54.5m (59¾yd) in Stone Grey or
   Natural (colour 1)*
Niroma Studio 5mm Single Twisted
Cotton String:
   9.5m (10½yd) in Sea Glass or
   Antique Peach (colour 2)*
6.5-cm (2½-in) gold metal ring
Sharp pair of scissors
Measuring tape or ruler
Optional: S-hook and garment rail

* Alternate colour variation shown
   on page 68.

SIZE

100cm (39½in) from the top of the
   ring to the bottom of the fringe,
   when empty

KNOTS

Gathering Knot (GK)
Left Facing Half Square (LHSQ)
Cord Alternating Square (CASQ)
Square (SQ)
Alternating Square (ASQ)
Reverse Lark's Head (RLH)

Tip:
Hang the metal ring up on a hook
to do this project. This will help
to keep the tension consistent and
you can easily check to see that the
sinnets are lining up nicely. You may
want to stand while working on the
top part and then sit on a chair once
you reach the bottom part in order
to keep your eyes in line with the
section that you are working on.

This plant hanger is adorned with a full bottom fringe that will dress up any space with its stylish and unique look. The long, soft strands of cotton string will swing about elegantly when a gentle breeze sways it from side to side. Pair it with a locally made pottery plant pot, a wooden fruit bowl or a vase to hold a bouquet of flowers. If you prefer a more traditional plant hanger without a bottom fringe, then you can omit the last step in the instructions (see the very first page of this book). This plant hanger looks best when holding a plant pot that's 10–15cm (4–6in) in diameter.

1. Cut three 4.8-m (5¼-yd) lengths of rope in colour 1 and three 3.2-m (3½-yd) lengths of rope in colour 2. Fold the ropes in half and place them through the metal ring so that each cord hangs evenly over both sides of the ring. You should have twelve cords hanging down.

2. Cut one 60-cm (23½-in) rope in colour 1 and tie a 3.5-cm (1½-in) GK around all of the cords hanging below the metal ring.

3. Using two colour 1 cords as Working Cords (WCs) and two colour 2 cords as Filler Cords (FC), tie fifty LHSQs to make a sinnet. Repeat this step twice more to create two more sinnets with the other cords.

4. Drop down 3cm (1¼in) and tie a CASQ. Tie eleven more SQs in the sinnet, using the colour 2 cords as the WCs and the colour 1 cords as the FCs. Repeat this step twice more with the other two sinnets.

5. Place two of the sinnets side by side so that the bottom SQs line up. Measure down 12.5cm (5in) and tie one ASQ with the hanging cords from both sinnets to join them together. Tie four more SQs. Repeat this step twice more to join all three sinnets together.

6. Cut one 60-cm (23½-in) rope in colour 1. Measure down 5cm (2in) and tie a 3.5-cm (1½-in) GK around all of the cords. Trim the cords 20cm (8in) below the GK.

7. To make the bottom fringe, cut sixty 65-cm (26-in) ropes in colour 1. Fold each rope in half and attach to the cords below each sinnet that connect to make a V-shape with RLHs. Each V-shape should hold twenty RLH cords, ten on each side.

FRINGED PLANT HANGER

Table runner

YOU WILL NEED:
Createaholic 2.5mm 3-ply cotton rope:
   176.4m (193yd) in Natural
Sharp pair of scissors
Measuring tape or ruler
Masking tape
Garment rail or dowel

SIZE
21 x 242cm (8¼ x 95¼in)

KNOTS
Lark's Head (LH)
Square (SQ)
Double Half Hitch (DHH)
Alternating Square (ASQ)

I have so many treasured memories of enjoying delicious homecooked meals, meaningful conversations and late nights filled with laughter with my nearest and dearest, all while sitting around the dinner table. Bring a little *hygge* to your next gathering with this beautiful table runner, and try accessorizing it with beeswax tapers in vintage brass holders and natural elements such as flowers or branches.

1. Cut twenty 8.9-m (9¾-yd) lengths of rope. Wrap each of the cut ends with a small piece of masking tape to prevent the rope from unravelling. Fold the ropes in half and attach to a garment rail or supporting dowel with LHs.

2. Measure down 25cm (10in) from the LHs and tie a SQ with C19–C22. Continue tying increasing open ASQs with all cords to make an upside-down V-shape. Repeat the pattern to create a second upside-down V-shape of increasing open ASQs directly below the first one.

3. Measure down 8cm (3in) from the middle point of the upside-down V-shape and repeat the pattern from Step 2 to make two upside-down V-shapes of increasing open ASQs.

4. Measure down 8cm (3in) from the middle point of the upside-down V-shape. C20 becomes the Holding Cord (HC). Tie DHHs onto the HC with C21–C40, moving from left to right to form a Downward Diagonal Line (DDL). C20 becomes the HC. Tie DHHs onto the HC with C19–C1, moving from right to left to form a DDL.

5. Measure down 8cm (3in) from the middle point of the upside-down V-shape and tie a SQ with C19–C22. Continue to tie increasing open ASQs with all cords to form an upside-down V-shape. Tie a SQ with C13–C16 and C25–C28 and then continue tying decreasing open ASQs to close the small diamond shape. Tie ASQs with C5–C8 and C17–C20 and then continue tying decreasing open ASQs to close the small diamond shape. Tie ASQs with C21–C24 and C33–C36 and then continue tying decreasing open ASQs to close the small diamond shape. Tie ASQs with C13–C16 and C25–C28 and then continue tying decreasing open ASQs to close the small diamond shape. Tie ASQs with C3–C6 and C35–C38 and then continue tying decreasing open ASQs to close the V-shape.

Project continues overleaf

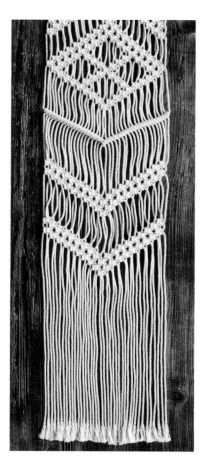

6. Measure down 5cm (2in) from the SQs on the far right and left and tie SQs with C1–C4 and C37–C40. Continue tying decreasing open ASQs with all cords to make a V-shape. Tie a second V-shape of ASQs with all cords directly below the one above.

7. Repeat Step 6.

8. C1 becomes the HC. Measure down 8cm (3in) from the SQ on the far left and tie DHHs onto the HC with C2–C20, moving from left to right to form a DDL. C40 becomes the HC. Measure down 8cm (3in) from the SQ on the far right and tie DHHs onto the HC with C39–C20, moving from right to left to form a DDL. Make SQs with C1–C4 and C37–C40 and then continue tying decreasing open ASQs with the rest of the cords to make a V-shape directly below the DHHs.

9. Measure down 5cm (2in) from the SQ on the far left and right and tie SQs with C1–C4 and C37–C40. Continue tying decreasing open ASQs with the rest of the cords to make a V-shape. Tie two more V-shapes of ASQs directly below the one above.

10. Repeat Step 9. Continuing from the last ASQ in the V-shape, tie increasing open ASQs with all of the cords to make the lower half of the X-shape.

11. Continue the pattern from Step 10 with increasing open ASQs twice more to complete a symmetrical X-shape. This completes the X-shape that is the centre of the table runner. From this point on, the pattern will mirror the other side of the X-shape.

12. Measure down 5cm (2in) from the middle ASQ (C19–C22) and tie a SQ with C19–C22. Continue tying increasing open ASQs with all of the cords to make an upside-down V-shape. Repeat the pattern two more times for a total of three upside-down V-shapes, one directly below the other.

13. Measure down 5cm (2in) from the middle ASQ (C19–C22) and tie a SQ with C19–C22. Continue tying increasing open ASQs with all of the cords to make an upside-down V-shape. C20 becomes the HC. Tie DHHs onto the HC with C21–C40, moving from left to right to form a DDL. C20 becomes the HC. Tie DHHs onto the HC with C19–C1, moving from right to left to form a DDL.

14. Measure down 8cm (3in) from the middle point of the upside-down V-shape and tie a SQ with C19–C22. Continue tying increasing open ASQs with all of the cords to make an upside-down V-shape. Make a second upside-down V-shape of increasing open ASQs directly below the one you just made.

15. Measure down 5cm (2in) from the middle ASQ (C19–C22) and repeat the pattern from Step 14 to make two upside-down V-shapes.

16. Repeat Step 15, skipping the last two ASQs on each side of the second up-side-down V-shape (C1–C4 and C37–C40).

17. Make an ASQ with C13–C16 and C25–C28 and then continue tying decreasing open ASQs to close the small diamond shape. Tie an ASQ with C5–C8 and C17–C20 and then continue tying decreasing open ASQs to close the small diamond shape. Tie an ASQ with C21–C24 and C33–C36 and then continue tying decreasing open ASQs to close the small diamond shape. Continue tying decreasing open ASQs to close the bottom middle diamond shape.

18. C1 becomes the HC. Measure down 8cm (3in) from the SQ on the far left and tie DHHs onto the HC with C2–C20, moving from left to right to form a DDL. C40 becomes the HC. Measure down 8cm (3in) from the SQ on the far right and tie DHHs onto the HC with C39–C20, moving from right to left to form a DDL.

19. Measure down 8cm (3in) from C1 and C40 and tie SQs with C1–C4 and C37–C40. Continue tying decreasing open ASQs with all cords to make a V-shape. Repeat once more to make a second V-shape with ASQs.

20. Repeat Step 19.

21. Remove the table runner from the garment rail or supporting dowel by cutting through the middle of the LHs.

22. Fold the table runner in half and trim the fringe so that both ends match, approximately 28cm (11in) from the bottom ASQs – or trim the fringe shorter, if you prefer.

Tip:
You can shorten the length of this table runner by trimming the fringe shorter than the recommendation of 28cm (11in). Unravel the cut ends on the fringe for extra charm.

Garland

YOU WILL NEED
Mary Maker Studio 5mm Cotton
String:
   111.2m (121¾yd) in Nude
Sharp pair of scissors
Measuring tape or ruler
Optional: tape
Optional: garment rail and S-hooks

SIZE
113 x 53cm (44½ x 21in)

KNOTS
Lark's Head (LH)
Square (SQ)
Alternating Square (ASQ)
Double Half Hitch (DHH)
Reverse Double Half Hitch (RDHH)
Overhand Loop Knot (OLK)
Gathering Knot (GK)

Create this versatile and festive garland that can hang across a fireplace mantel, above a crib in your baby's room or behind a dessert table, or use it as a photobooth backdrop at your next party. The long, uneven fringe complements the details along the top of the garland and adds just the right amount of texture. This project may look complicated, but it is relatively easy to do because the design repeats itself across the entire length of the garland.

1. Cut one 150-cm (60-in) rope and sixty-six 165-cm (65-in) ropes. The 150-cm (60-in) rope will be the Supporting Cord that the Working Cord (WC) will be attached to – this takes the place of the dowel or driftwood used in other projects. Fold the 165-cm (65-in) ropes in half and attach to the Supporting Cord with LHs. The LHs should be centred on the Supporting Cord and side by side. Leave the ends of the Supporting Cord off to the side until you reach Step 9.

2. Tie a row of SQs with all of the cords attached to the Supporting Cord.

3. Starting with the first three SQs on the left, continue tying decreasing ASQs to make an upside-down triangle shape. C12 becomes the Holding Cord (HC). Tie DHHs onto the HC with C11–C7, moving from right to left to form a Downward Diagonal Line (DDL). C1 becomes the HC. Tie DHHs onto the HC with C2–C7, moving from left to right to form a DDL. Repeat the pattern across the entire length of the garland to make eleven sections.

4. Tie a SQ with C11–C14 that measures 1cm (½in) down from the DHHs on either side. Repeat the pattern across the entire garland.

Project continues overleaf

Tip:
You can tie the 150-cm (60-in) rope to a garment rail or tape the ends down to a flat working surface to hold it in place while you work on the design.

5. Starting from the SQs you made in Step 4, continue tying increasing open ASQs along the DHHs, spaced approximately 5mm (¼in) away from the DHHs. The ASQs should form a zig-zag pattern across the entire length of the garland. Repeat the pattern once more to form another zig-zag of ASQs, one directly below the other.

6. C12 becomes the HC. Tie DHHs onto the HC with C11–C7, moving from right to left to form a DDL. C1 becomes the HC. Tie DHHs onto the HC with C2–C7, moving from left to right to form a DDL. Repeat the pattern once more so that there are two V-shapes of DHHs. C12 becomes the HC. Tie RDHHs onto the HC with C11–C7, moving from right to left to form a DDL. C1 becomes the HC. Tie RDHHs onto the HC with C2–C7, moving from left to right to form a DDL.

7. Repeat the pattern from Step 6 across the entire length of the garland.

8. Using a fine-toothed comb, gently brush out 2cm (¾in) of the cut ends of the cords (see page 69).

9. Tie OLKs at both ends of the Supporting Cord, 10cm (4in) away from the LHs. Ensure the OLKs are tied tightly. Trim the excess cord 2cm (¾in) below the OLK.

10. Cut a 40-cm (16-in) rope and tie a 3-cm (1¼-in) GK below the OLK. Repeat this step on the opposite side.

GARLAND

PROJECTS

Large statement piece

YOU WILL NEED

Rope Shop 3mm Cotton 3
Strand Rope:

    245.2m (268yd) in Natural

122-cm (48-in) wooden dowel or
    driftwood with 2.5-cm (1-in)
    diameter

Sharp pair of scissors

Measuring tape or ruler

Masking tape

Optional: cotton fabric dye and
    dyeing tools

Optional: garment rail and S-hooks

SIZE

122 x 76.5cm (48 x 30in)

KNOTS

Lark's Head (LH)
Square (SQ)
Alternating Square (ASQ)
Reverse Lark's Head (RLH)
Double Half Hitch (DHH)
Gathering Knot (GK)

Tip:
Rope Shop measures the thickness
of their rope when it is pulled tightly.
Most other brands measure the
thickness of their rope when it is
relaxed; therefore, if you are using
loosely wound rope, I recommend
using 4mm rope for this project.
Wrap each of the cut ends with
a small piece of masking tape to
prevent the rope from unravelling.

Believe me when I tell you that this statement piece is going to completely transform your room. This one was designed to hang over your bed but will also look gorgeous above a couch or sideboard, in a large entryway or in a window. Don't let the size intimidate you – this project is easy to create. The key with this one is to keep the measurements precise and to maintain symmetry and consistent tension throughout the project. If you are going to dip-dye your wall hanging, then I strongly encourage you to carefully follow the manufacturer's dye instructions and to choose a product that is suitable for cotton.

1. Cut twelve 3.3-m (3¾-yd) lengths of rope. Fold the ropes in half and attach to the dowel with LHs. The ropes should be centred on the dowel and should sit side by side.

2. Tie SQs with C5–C8, C9–C12, C13–C16 and C17–C20.

3. Tie SQs with C1–C4 and C21–C24 and then continue tying decreasing open ASQs to make a V-shape.

4. Repeat Step 3.

5. C24 becomes the Holding Cord (HC). Tie DHHs onto the HC with C23–C13, moving from right to left to form a Downward Diagonal Line (DDL). C1 becomes the HC. Tie DHHs onto the HC with C2–C13, moving from left to right to form a DDL.

6. Measure 7cm (2¾in) down from the DHHs above C1 and C24, then repeat Step 3.

7. Repeat Step 5 and Step 3.

8. Tie ASQs with C9–C12, C7–C10, C13–C16 and C15–C18 and then continue tying decreasing open ASQs to close the diamond shape.

9. C18 becomes the HC. Tie DHHs onto the HC with C17–C13, moving from right to left to form a DDL. C7 becomes the HC. Tie DHHs onto the HC with C8–C13, moving from left to right to form a DDL.

Project continues overleaf

10. Measure 15cm (6in) down from the SQs above C1 and C24, then repeat Step 3, 4, 5 and 6. Trim the cords 13cm (5in) below the last sequence of knots.

11. Cut eight 2.8-m (3-yd) lengths of rope. Fold the ropes in half and attach to the dowel with LHs on the left side of the section you just created, leaving a 7-cm (2¾-in) space.

12. Tie a row of SQs and then continue tying decreasing ASQs to make an upside-down triangle shape.

13. C8 becomes the HC. Measure down 2.5cm (1in) and tie DHHs onto the HC with C9–C16, moving from left to right to form a DDL. C8 becomes the HC. Tie DHHs onto the HC with C7–C1, moving from right to left to form a DDL.

14. Tie SQs with C7–C10, C5–C8, C9–C12, C3–C6 and C11–C14 and then continue tying decreasing open ASQs to close the diamond shape.

15. C16 becomes the HC. Tie DHHs onto the HC with C15–C9, moving from right to left to form a DDL. C1 becomes the HC. Tie DHHs onto the HC with C2–C9, moving from left to right to form a DDL. Repeat this step one more time.

16. Tie a SQ with C1–C4 and C13–C16 and then continue to tie decreasing ASQs to close the V-shape.

17. Measure 7cm (2¾in) down from the SQs above C1 and C16 and tie SQs with C1–C4 and C13–C16. Continue tying decreasing open ASQs to close the V-shape.

18. Repeat Steps 15 and 16. Trim the cords 13cm (5in) below the last sequence of knots.

19. Repeat Steps 11–18 on the right side of the middle section.

20. Cut twelve 165-cm (65-in) lengths of rope. Fold the ropes in half and attach to the dowel with LHs on the right side of the section you just created, leaving a 7-cm (2¾-in) space. Repeat Repeat Steps 2, 3, 4, 5, 6 and 5. Trim the cords 13cm (5in) below the last sequence of knots.

21. Repeat Step 20 on the left side of the wall hanging.

22. Cut eight 150-cm (59-in) lengths of rope. Make two bundles of four ropes (see page 76). Line up the cut ends in each bundle and drape the bundles evenly over the dowel on both sides of the middle section. Cut two 160-cm (63-in) lengths of rope and use each piece to tie a 10-cm (4-in) GK to secure the ropes to the dowel. Unravel the cords below the GK and trim to clean up any uneven ends. Position the bundles evenly between sections.

23. Cut eight 120-cm (47¼-in) ropes. Make two bundles of four ropes. Line up the cut ends in each of the bundles, drape the bundles evenly over the dowel in between panels 1 and 2, and 4 and 5. Cut two 160-cm (63-in) ropes and use each piece to tie a 10-cm (4-in) GK to secure the ropes to the dowel. Unravel the cords below the GK and trim to clean up any uneven ends. Position the bundles evenly between sections.

24. Cut one 3.3-m (3¾-yd) rope. Secure the rope to both ends of the dowel with LHs, making sure that the ends of the ropes hang evenly on both sides and that the rope hangs to 24cm (9½in) below the middle point of the dowel (it will hang slightly lower once the cords have been attached). Tie DHHs at both ends to hold the rope in place. This rope becomes the Supporting Cord, which takes the place of the dowel or driftwood used in other projects.

25. Cut ninety 100-cm (39½-in) ropes. If you are dyeing the fringe, see note below. Fold the ropes in half and attach to the Supporting Cord with RLHs to fill the entire length of the cord. Don't tape the ends of the cut rope, as the ends should unravel a little bit on their own to create texture. Trim the ends of the Supporting Cord to match the length of the other cords.

Note: Once the ropes have been cut, bundle them into three groups and line up the cut ends in each bundle. Tie the ropes together with a piece of string or yarn at 50cm (20in) – the middle point. Fold each bundle in half and proceed with dip-dyeing the cut ends evenly on both sides, as per the dye instructions. Let the ropes dry completely before attaching them.

26. Gently move the big fringe behind the other sections and long tassels.

Feathers

Short pieces of string (scraps
   left over from other projects
   are perfect)
One longer string for each feather
Sharp pair of scissors
Measuring tape or ruler
Fine-toothed comb or wire
   bristle brush
Optional: rotary cutter and
   cutting mat
Optional: fabric stiffening spray
   or strong-hold hair spray
Optional: felt with adhesive backing

As you finish the projects in this book, your pile of scraps is going to start adding up. Don't throw them out! There are plenty of ways that you can use them, including these pretty feathers. You may be excited to get started on this project right away, but I recommend that you wait until you have a nice collection of small pieces and save your roll of string for the bigger projects. You may leave the feathers soft and loose or stiffen them up with a fabric stiffening spray and adhesive felt. You will decide on the size, shape, colour and level of sturdiness – I will simply teach you the basics and then you can choose the rest.

1. Decide how long you want your feather to be and how long you want the cord it hangs from to be. Once you have decided, cut a piece of rope twice the total desired length. For example, if you want the feather to be 15cm (6in) long and the string it hangs from to be 10cm (4in) long, add these lengths together (25cm/10in) and double it – cutting a 50-cm (20-in) rope. Fold the rope in half and lay it on a flat surface. This rope becomes the Holding Cord (HC).

2. Decide how wide you want the feather to be. Once you have decided on the width, cut two ropes to match that measurement, plus 3cm (1¼in). For example, if the width is going to be approximately 12cm (4¾in) across, cut two 15-cm (6-in) ropes. These ropes become Working Cords (WCs).

3. Fold the first WC in half. Slide the folded end under and 2–3cm (¾–1¼in) past the HC. You will be working from the top of the feather down to the bottom, so make sure you start at the correct measurement. For example, if you want a 15-cm (6-in) feather, place the first WC under the HC at 15cm (6in).

4. Fold the second WC in half. Put the folded end under and up through the first WC's folded end, going over the HC in the opposite direction to the first WC. Gently lift the first WC's cut ends up and through the folded end of the second WC.

Project continues overleaf

5. Pull the cut ends of both WCs to tighten the knot around the HC. You may have to straighten the HC after pulling the knot closed. The knot will resemble a Square Knot (SQ) and the cut ends should lie evenly on opposite sides of the HC.

6. Repeat Steps 2–5, moving from the top of the feather down towards the bottom. Alternate the direction that the WCs are being added in; for example, if you slid the first WC under the HC going from top to bottom on the first knot, go from bottom to top on the second knot, and so on. Stop adding WCs at least a few centimetres (an inch or so) from the cut ends of the HC, as this will make the tip of the feather.

7. Ensure that the knots are tied tightly and that they are close together. Once you have the desired shape and size, gently brush out all of the WCs with a fine-toothed comb (see page 69).

8. Decide whether you want a loose and soft feather or one that is stiff and holds its shape. If you want it to be loose, trim the feather to the desired shape with a sharp pair of scissors or a rotary cutter and mat. For a stiff appearance, spray one side of the feather with a fabric stiffening spray or hair spray of your choice and then lay it flat to dry. Once it has dried completely, flip it over and spray the other side and let it dry. Trim the feather to the desired shape with a sharp pair of scissors or a rotary cutter and mat. You can add additional support by cutting a piece of adhesive felt that is slightly smaller than the feather and then attaching it to the back. You are now ready to hang your feather up on a wall, dowel or a piece of driftwood. It can easily be secured to another object by adding a Gathering Knot (GK) so that it holds its position.

Tip:
If you want a precise cut when trimming the shape, be sure to use very sharp scissors or a rotary cutter and cutting mat. When brushing out the string, you may find that little fibres become airborne and may tickle your nose. I recommend wearing a mask over your mouth and nose to prevent you from breathing in the fibres.

Reference

Displaying your work

At long last, your project is finished and you are finally ready to install your masterpiece in its new home – hooray! While you were tying knot after knot, you were probably visualizing how your macramé was going to look once it was finished and hanging up on your wall. Trust me when I say that this exciting moment of finishing a project and installing it does not get old, and it is actually very addictive.

Do yourself a favour and take your time to find the perfect spot to hang your macramé. If you can, have someone hold your project up while you stand back to see if you like the position before you put a nail in the wall.

Once your masterpiece is hanging proudly on the wall, you will want to tidy it up a little bit since the cords may have become dishevelled from the move between your workspace and its new home. The easiest way to tidy up any fringe and other loose cords is to use your fingers to comb them out, starting from the top and then gently pulling them in a downward direction. Another way to tidy up the loose cords is to place a few cords in between your middle finger and index finger, and then gently pull the cords through your fingers in a downward direction. I find that a combination of these two methods works really well. You may also want to have your comb or brush close by so that you can tidy up any pieces of rope or string that you had previously brushed out.

If the overall shape of the design has retracted from storing it, rolling it up or for another reason, then you can give it a gentle tug to adjust the knotted areas to straighten them out. Start by giving a very soft tug and then gradually increase the tension if necessary to move the knotted areas back to their original position. It is unlikely that you will have to do this unless the project has been rolled up.

Maintenance

Your macramé creations require very little maintenance, and for the most part they should not need regular cleaning. If your macramé is installed in a spot that tends to get dusty, then perhaps a light dusting every once in a while may be necessary to keep it looking its best. Unless your wall hanging has been overhandled or it has obvious dirt, dust or stains on it, I do not recommend that you clean it. If something unfortunate happens and it must be cleaned, then it should be spot cleaned using minimal product and handled with extra care. Never put your macramé in a washing machine, even on a delicate cycle.

STORING MACRAMÉ

There may come a time when you have to take a macramé wall hanging down and roll it up to store it or to ship it. For the most part, this is fairly easy to do without damaging the design. To do so safely, you will need something large enough to lay your entire project down on top of that can also be rolled up. Eco-friendly postal wrapping paper, corrugated cardboard wrap or even a bedsheet, towel, tablecloth or blanket will work well for this. Avoid using materials that are darker in colour than your rope or string, since the dye may transfer onto your project.

Lay your packaging material down on a flat surface, and then carefully lay your macramé down on top of it. Straighten out the cords as much as possible and tuck in any loose ends so that everything is held together. Starting at the top where the dowel or driftwood is, carefully roll the piece up along with the packing material, keeping all of the cords as straight and tidy as possible. Once it has been completely rolled up, wrap a few pieces of twine or string around it to hold it together and to prevent it from unrolling. Once it has been rolled up, it will easily slide into a shipping box or it can be stored as is.

Beyond this book

Once you have completed the projects in this book and you feel comfortable with the various knots and techniques, you will be able to move on to creating your own original designs. This is absolutely the best part of learning how to macramé.

If it seems a little daunting, you could begin by putting your own spin on familiar projects. You could add a variety of coloured strings to the Mug Rugs and Plant Rugs projects or try adding a second dip-dyed fringe to hang across the entire length of the Large Statement Piece. Have fun and play around with different textures, unconventional materials and colour combinations.

Every once in a while, I start a new project and about halfway through I get stuck and cannot decide on my next move. When this happens, I find it helpful to take a step back and to look at the project from a distance and from different angles. There is nothing wrong with taking a break and walking away until you are once again feeling inspired and ready to continue. Sometimes it only takes a couple of hours, and sometimes it takes a couple of months. There is no expiration date on your materials, and therefore, there is no rush to complete a project.

You can find tons of inspirational photos online that will help you to get started on a new project if you are having a hard time knowing where to begin. What you could do is use one or possibly two elements from a design that you love, and then let your creativity flow and dream up something magical and unique for your own piece. One of the pleasures of doing macramé is starting a project not knowing what the end result will be, and just enjoying the journey from beginning to end. There are also plenty of patterns available to purchase online if you prefer step-by-step instructions.

When you are working on a brand-new design, I encourage you to keep a notebook close by, so that you can write down the pertinent information that you will need to recreate it in the future. Write down the dimensions of the piece, the length of the cords that were cut for each section, and the type of rope that you used, including the colour, thickness and brand. You will thank yourself for taking this extra step now as it will ultimately save you time in the future.

There are a number of online communities for macramé makers and admirers to join if you are looking to talk with others who are experienced in the craft. In these groups you can ask questions, learn new techniques, discover new fibre artists, find suppliers, learn about events or ask for opinions. There are so many kind and wonderful people who are more than happy to help and offer advice to anyone who is looking.

Index

Acknowledgements

First and foremost, I want to acknowledge my husband who is the most incredible person and partner I could have asked for. Thank you, Jody, for your love and support and solid advice. There is no way that I would have been able to write this book had you not been the most amazing partner who went above and beyond in our day-to-day life so that I could take the time I needed to work on this project.

To my dear children, Daniel and Jacob, who motivate me to be the best version of myself every day. I love you both with all my heart.

To my family and friends, thank you for being so supportive over the years. I appreciate each and every one of you who has offered helping hands, materials, ideas and words of encouragement and I am truly thankful to have all of you in my life.

To my Commissioning Editor, Ellie Corbett, who first reached out to ask if I would be interested in writing this book. Thank you so much for believing in me and for giving me this wonderful opportunity. It has been an absolute pleasure working with you.

To my Editor, Rachel Silverlight, who has been incredibly supportive throughout this entire process. I am grateful to have had the opportunity to work with you on this project and I want to thank you for all of your hard work and patience as we went back and forth during the editing process.

To the team of brilliant individuals at Ilex and Octopus Publishing who were involved with this book: Alison Starling, Ellen Sandford O'Neill, Ben Gardiner, Caroline Alberti, Lucy Carter and Nic Jones. Thank you so much for your time and effort to make this book a success. I feel honoured to have had access to your talent.

I would also like to thank Tammy Kerr for the seamless design and layout, Caitlin Keegan for illustrating the various knots and techniques, Rachel Vere for styling each of the projects beautifully in order to be photographed, Lucy Sykes-Thompson from Studio Polka for her design expertise, and Kim Lightbody for all of the stunning photographs seen throughout the book.

And last but certainly not least, I want to acknowledge you! Thank you so much for picking up this book and allowing me to guide you on your macramé journey.

About the author

Tiffany Allen is a fibre artist with a passion for macramé, and the owner of Macramé and Driftwood. Her artwork is inspired by nature, movement, texture and colour and she finds great satisfaction in crafting pieces that add originality and interest to a room. She puts her creative heart into every one of her projects and she can often be found in her home studio dreaming up new designs and working on custom requests from clients from around the world. Tiffany lives in Thunder Bay, Ontario with her husband and two young children. For more about Tiffany, see: @macrameanddriftwood on Instagram, or visit www.macrameanddriftwood.com